*"What are the roots that clutch, what branches grow
Out of this stony rubbish?" (T. S. Elliot, The Waste Land)*

the Yam

Chic Scott
Dave Dornian
Ben Gadd

50 years of climbing on Yamnuska

Front cover top: Heinz Kahl leading the last pitch of *Red Shirt* during the first ascent. Photo Gunti Prinz.
Front cover bottom: the south face of Yamnuska.
Photo Lloyd Gallagher collection.

Back cover: Yamnuska emerging from the mists.
Photo Chic Scott.

Title page: *Jazz Beat of the Nun's Groove.* Jeff Everett on the crux 3rd pitch. Photo Glenn Reisenhofer.
Inset: Hans Gmoser below Yamnuska.
Courtesy Urs Kallen collection.

Contents page: Brian Wyvill on the 4th pitch of *Bringers of the Dawn*. Photo Greg Fletcher.

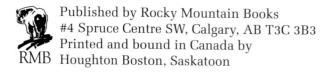
Published by Rocky Mountain Books
#4 Spruce Centre SW, Calgary, AB T3C 3B3
Printed and bound in Canada by
Houghton Boston, Saskatoon

We acknowledge the financial support of the Government of Canada through the Book Publishing Industry Development Program (BPIDP) for our publishing activities.

National Library of Canada Cataloguing in Publication Data

Scott, Chic, 1945-
  The Yam : 50 years of climbing on Yamnuska / Chic Scott, Dave Dornian, Ben Gadd

  Includes index.
  ISBN 0-921102-97-6

  1. Mountaineering--Alberta--Yamnuska, Mount--Guidebooks. 2. Yamnuska, Mount (Alta.)--Guidebooks. I. Dornian, Dave, 1955- II. Gadd, Ben, 1946- III. Title.
GV199.44.C22A4585 2003   796.52'2'09712332   C2003-910216-5

Contents

Introduction

From the Trans-Canada Highway, Yam looks unlikely and unloved—a bit of biscuit tipped up on a hillcrest to the north as you drive toward the bigger and more impressive lumps to the west. Not the highest, definitely. Not the most alpine looking, either. Many nearby peaks offer more-pointed and precipitous summits.

Yet, as you drive toward it, along the 1X and then back east a short way on the 1A, the slope heaves up and rears overhead. You twist your wheel left onto the gravel and find the parking lot and the bathrooms of the newly organized Bow Valley Wildland Provincial Park.

If you follow the trail signage, an hour later you can stand on the ridge line east of the rock face and just plain have an entirely different experience. Up close and personal like this, the face of Yamnuska runs by you like a freight train of Dolomite that's a mile long. Its walls rake the sky as it curls to the west—a cereal–coloured Cinemascope curtain tracing a tumbling ogee over the scree.

If you stand this way, rooted in a sense of wonder as you watch Yamnuska's train come round the curve, you're not the first. The vision has inspired many to reach out and place their penny on the rails.

Dave Dornian

Clouds breaking around Yamnuska.
Photo Chic Scott

Foreword

I was introduced to Yamnuska in 1956 while reading all I could find out about the Canadian mountains. Hans Gmoser had written many articles on face routes up this amazing cliff. I was intrigued.

My relationship was established in 1959 when I hiked up and over the summit from the back. Sitting alone at the top, I filled my head with thoughts of one day ascending the routes spreading out below me.

By the Sixties the relationship had blossomed into an all-out affair, although I was not her only lover. The mountain challenged me and other devotees to go further and harder than we thought our skills and equipment could go. Yamnuska forced us out of the norm and made us the leaders we became.

Climbing there up to 50 times each season, we became intimate and familiar with the various qualities and difficulties all along the vertical landscape. Many days and nights were spent sitting with others, but always alone, watching how the light continued to form the varied Yam moods. How shadows brought out revealed features—the lines of future adventure. What emotions were evoked by the texture of the gray prickly rock, or the lighter yellow, sometimes warm with sun, sometimes cold and slick, but always a welcome stimulus, a needed bond feeding our motivation.

This was our mountain. My mountain. She became a personal symbol as I felt a sense of ownership being bestowed upon me. I was protective and a bit jealous, but at the same time I wanted everyone to know the level of what we were doing and to realize their own potential.

It wasn't long before a new generation of younger, bolder climbers started to cut their teeth on this rock and I began to realize that we were only temporary caretakers. The standards we had set were being rewritten.

Forty years have passed, and Yam is still a training ground for the climbers of tomorrow. I still climb there occasionally; such is the magnetism and romantic allure she holds for me and the Canadian climbing tapestry.

What a place—what a time—the meaning of existence—a partial reality of life.

Don Vockeroth

West End

Necromancer

CMC Wall

Suicide Wall

Bottleneck
Kahl Wall
Red Shirt
The Bowl
Yellow Edge
East End

the Yam

Top: morning mists on Yamnuska, showing main climbing areas. Photo William Marler.

Right: Yamnuska from Goat Mountain. Photo Rod Plasman.

Opposite: evening light on Yamnuska. Courtesy Lloyd Gallagher collection.

Climber's camp below Yamnuska. Photo Rob Owens

Painting the pumpkin on *Unnamed*, 1968. Photo Ron Robinson.

Opposite: Larry Stanier on the bolt ladder of
Corkscrew. Photo Grant Statham.

Steve DeMaio on 4th pitch of *East End Boys.* Photo Andy Genereux.

Marlboro cigarette ad from *Vogue* magazine, September 1997. Courtesy Maja Swannie.

Gandalf fighting the Balrog. Painting by Billy Davidson, courtesy Perry Davis.

13

1 Setting the Scene

Ben Gadd

Yamnuska will catch your eye as you drive the Trans-Canada Highway between Banff and Calgary. There it is, a great block of gray-and-tan Cambrian limestone north of the road, high up and sitting apart from the other peaks at the mountain front.

What turns the head of travellers is the south face of the mountain. It's a big cliff, a kilometre and a half long and 360 m high at the summit, elevation 2235 m above sea level. That cliff is so straight, so sheer, that the locals who live below it on the Stoney Indian Reserve call it "the flat-faced mountain," which is what "Yamnuska" means in Stoney (Sioux). In English the usual pronunciation is "Yam-NUSS-ka." But in Sioux the spelling is "Îyâmnathka," pronounced with a leading long "e" sound. The third syllable is given a "th" sound, so it comes out "Ee-yum-NOTH-ka."

On current maps, the spelling is not "Yamnuska" but "Îyâmnathka." Coupled to that is another name entirely—"Laurie"—resulting in a rather long map label: "Mount Laurie (Îyâmnathka)." What's with "Laurie"? Read on.

Above: Ben Gadd. Photo Gillean Daffern.
Opposite: Jeff Moore on *Boomerang*. Photo Brian Spear.

The Landscape
What the Hunters Saw

Yamnuska must have had other names, for human eyes have been drawn to it for at least 11,000 years. Not far away, at Sibbald Flats in what is today Kananaskis Country, archeologists have found evidence of occupation by the oldest known culture in Canada. The aboriginals who camped at Sibbald Flats ate a lot of elk, deer and bighorn sheep. They killed those animals with spears, each tipped with the distinctively fashioned Clovis point.

No doubt these tribespeople also patrolled the grassy meadows along the Bow River in search of bison. This would have brought them close to Yamnuska. Perhaps, on one of those trips, a party of hunters walked below Yamnuska's awesome south face. Perhaps someone in that party delighted in the ravens and the prairie falcons and the golden eagles riding the updrafts above the mountain. Perhaps that person attempted a climb. Maybe a small group of friends headed up together. Then as now, bighorn trails must have led to the summit. There is no reason to doubt that given good weather those early mountaineers reached the top.

> *"There is no reason to doubt that given good weather those early mountaineers reached the top."*

The view from the summit back then was missing the human clutter seen in the Bow Valley today: roads, railway, Kananaskis Dam and its small reservoir at Seebe, Horseshoe Dam and another reservoir a few kilometres downstream, high-tension power lines leading from the dams' generators, Ghost Reservoir farther east, quarries for shale and gravel and sandstone, a gas station, a provincial park campground, scattered dwellings, the village of Morley and other clusters of buildings. Remove all that and imagine the aboriginal climbers as they reached the crest of the peak. Imagine their guts tightening and their eyes widening as they crept to the very edge of the precipice and gazed far, far down.

Below them lay the valley, wide and green. Running along its centre was the river. In midsummer the Bow would have been tinted powder blue, just as it is today, by countless tiny particles of rock carried away from dozens of glaciers rasping away at the Rockies upstream. But here there were none. The last major glaciation had ended a thousand years before, and the place had reforested itself.

The first summiters might have spoken excitedly to one another as they peered down at the ponds on the valley floor. They would have noted the low hills rising above the ponds and the low ridges snaking around them. They might have agreed to check out those little water bodies when they got back. There could be game there, and they could sneak up on it by using the hills and ridges.

It was at the end of a glacial period that these landforms were produced. A long glacier had extended from the Wapta Icefield, headwaters of the Bow River, all the way to this place, where it had spread out in a huge lobe that stretched from the base of Yamnuska to the other side of the valley. Under the ice, water was running through stream-cut tunnels, carrying sand and gravel along in the dark. When the glacier melted, these under-ice streamcourses were exposed as the low, winding gravel ridges seen by our Clovis hunters. The technical term for such ridges is "eskers."

Water was also flowing over the top of the melting ice sheet. Lots of water. Gravel dragged along in the rushing torrents covered and buried masses of glacial ice the size of city blocks. There the ice remained, protected from the sun, slowly melting away beneath the surface for hundreds of years. As the ice blocks melted, the land above them subsided into hollows left by the shrinking ice. Such depressions are properly termed "kettles." The lakes and ponds on the valley floor are kettles that hold water. The low hills represent just the opposite process: in places where the ice under the gravel was thin, the gravel had built up correspondingly thicker and remained as piles when the ice melted away. Such hills are called "kames," and they are often found as the high points between kettles. Such a landscape is termed "kame-and-kettle topography." The kame-and-kettle topography of the Bow Valley below Yamnuska is a classic example of what glacial ice and running water can produce in combination.

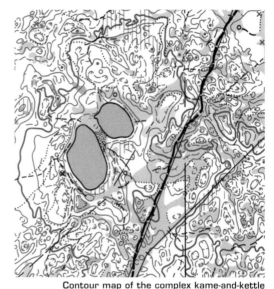

Contour map of the complex kame-and-kettle topography below Yamnuska
Contour interval 5 m, area covered one square kilometre. Courtesy Alberta Orienteering Association.

How melting glacial ice produced the topography below Yamnuska

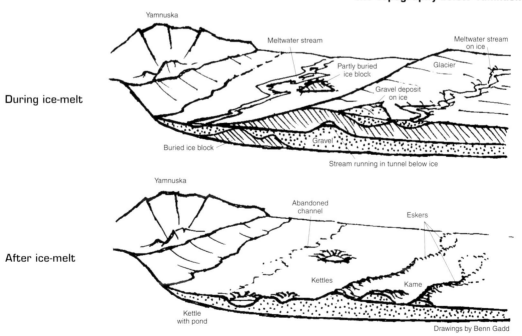

Drawings by Benn Gadd

"The ice was so thick it may have overtopped Yamnuska."

Glaciation in the Rockies

The Rockies before glaciation.

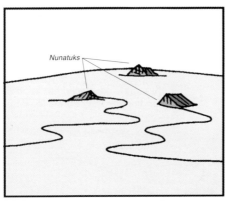

At the height of glaciation most peaks are covered by ice.

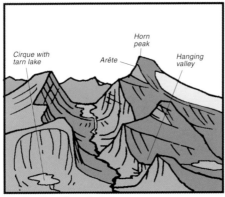

The Rockies after glaciation.

No one, not even the Clovis people, seems to have lived in the Rockies while all this was going on. It occurred before humans reached this part of North America, or at least before we have any strong evidence that they were here. Yet we know how the Bow Valley eskers and kettles and kames developed because these landforms look just like those produced today where large glaciers are melting. In geology, the present is the key to the past.

The ice ages of the Pleistocene Epoch, meaning the last two million years, left other gifts to the landscape around Yamnuska. The steepness and straightness of Yam's south face, so nicely arranged along the great ice-cut curve of the Bow Valley's north wall, must be largely a product of glacial erosion. During one or more big glacial advances, the ice flowing down the Bow Valley was so thick it may have overtopped Yamnuska. Car-size chunks of limestone were plucked from the mountain and carried eastward; today you'll find some of those erratics decorating the wooded ridge running east from the peak. Other advances, not as thick, ground away at the base of Yamnuska, causing frequent rockslides and steepening the cliff above. The north side of the mountain has a large, deep scoop—a classic glacial cirque—carved from it by Pleistocene ice.

About 7500 years ago the spear hunters gave way to a society that used atlatls (throwing sticks) to launch heavy darts at their prey. By about 2000 years ago hunters in the Bow Valley were using bow-and-arrow weapons. Then came the Kootenay people—or maybe it was the same bunch all along, just learning new skills—who were still there when North America was invaded by Europeans.

If the Kootenays had been able to remain in the Bow Valley through the onslaught, we would know the name they gave Yamnuska. Maybe they, too, called it "flat-faced mountain." However, they were driven out by enemy tribes carrying European firepower, and their descendants, now living on four small reserves in southeastern British Columbia, are unable to recall much about the old days in Alberta.

Stoney Indians riding across Morley Flats with Yamnuska in the distance at far right. Photo Elliot Barnes, courtesy Whyte Museum of the Canadian Rockies.

The Locals

"These Mountains are our Sacred Places"

The quote above is from Stoney Chief John Snow, and it is the Stoney First Nation that lives below Yamnuska now. The Stoneys are essentially Sioux who came from their heartland, Lake of the Woods on the Canadian Shield along the Manitoba/Ontario border. When Europeans brought disease and conflict to Central Canada, the Sioux split into various warring factions and a lot of them moved away. (Elsewhere than in the Rockies, these far-flung tribes are known as Nakoda, Lakota, Dakota and Assiniboine.) The Stoney branch of the wandering Sioux were able to fight, bargain and work their way west to the Rockies. They arrived in the Bow Valley in the mid-1700s, more or less.

The official history of the Stoney people, written by John Snow and published in 1977, disagrees with the foregoing. In Snow's view, the Stoneys have been living in the Rockies forever. Who is right? Take

your pick. At least it's easy to agree on the term "Stoney." This name recognizes the Sioux method of boiling meals by dropping hot stones into bags of meat and water.

The Stoneys coexisted uneasily with their fierce Blackfoot neighbors to the south. They got along better with their Cree neighbors to the north. When the Canadian government showed up bearing Treaty Seven for signature in 1877, the Stoneys were willing to cooperate. This treaty gave them their present reserve below Yamnuska.[1]

The 1877 treaty was offered to southern Alberta's aboriginal peoples mainly to defuse rising tensions and to secure right-of-way for the new Canadian Pacific Railway about to be built across the country in a hurry. The signatories included three First Nations: the Blackfoot Confederacy, the Tsuu T'ina (at that time called "Sarcees") and the Stoneys from the Bow River south. In 1882 the CPR's track was laid through the new Stoney reserve and on to Banff.

1. There are two other Sioux reserves in Alberta, both much smaller than this one: Eden Valley, along the Highwood River southwest of Calgary, and Bighorn, along the North Saskatchewan River east of Nordegg. Bighorn was established by Treaty Six.

Non-natives Arrive

"…we left our horses and went up along the River on Foot s15w 21/2m to a Point of the Mountain which we thought practicable, for the Mountain all this last Course presents an inaccessible Steep…" (David Thompson describing travelling up the Bow River valley on November 30, 1800. The "inaccessible Steep" refers to the cliffs of Yamnuska and Goat Mountain.)

David Thompson, the North West Company's most famous employee, explored the Bow Valley in 1800, guided by Kootenays. He may have been the first non-aboriginal person to see Yamnuska. Forced by hostile Blackfoot warriors to look elsewhere for his company's route to and from British Columbia, he eventually chose Athabasca Pass, much farther north in today's Jasper National Park. The Alberta Rockies were of little interest to the Nor'westers, in comparison to the fur-rich province-to-be across the divide. But in 1832 the Hudson's Bay Company, which had taken over the North West Company in 1821, built a trading post not far east of Yamnuska where Old Fort Creek joins the Bow River. Known as "Peigan Post" and also as "Old Bow Fort," the operation was harassed by Blackfoot warriors and received little trade. It was abandoned only two years later.

In August of 1858 the Palliser Expedition travelled through the Bow Valley, pass-

Site of Old Bow Fort c. 1910. Photo H. Pollard collection, courtesy Provincial Archives of Alberta.

ing south of Yamnuska. Led by Irish cavalry captain John Palliser, the purpose of this government-sponsored trip across western Canada was to ascertain the possibility of settlement. In his journal Palliser noted the ruins of Old Bow Fort, but did not mention Yamnuska.

In 1875 the Yamnuska area acquired its first notable non-native settlers, both from Ontario, then known as Upper Canada. The Rev. George McDougall was a Methodist missionary to the Stoneys, and his friend Andrew Sibbald was the band's first school-teacher. They both arrived in 1875, spent their careers mainly on the reserve and are buried there.

On the western boundary of the Stoney lands, along the north bank of the Bow directly south of Yamnuska, John Brewster started a homestead in the late 1800s for overwintering his dairy cattle. It remained in the family as the Kananaskis Ranch. On the other side of the river, the Rafter Six Ranch was founded at about the same time by horse fancier James Walker, a colonel in the North West Mounted Police (now the RCMP).

Around the turn of the 19th century, the Stoney reserve and other locations nearby in the Bow Valley below Yamnuska were home at times to some of the Rockies' better-known historical figures, including other members of the Brewster family, as well as Tom Lusk, Bill Potts, William Twin and Tom Wilson. They all became involved in what was then a brand-new business for the Canadian west: tourism, as practiced not far west of Yamnuska in Banff, where Canada's first national park was founded in 1885. Originally limited to a small area surrounding the hot springs on Sulphur Mountain, in 1902 the park was briefly expanded eastward to the Stoney Indian Reserve boundary at Kananaskis River, far enough east to include all of what was until recently the Yamnuska Natural Area. After further changes to the park's size, the National Parks Act of 1930 set the boundary as it is now, west of Canmore.

George McDougall. Courtesy Glenbow Archives.

James Walker. Photo Leo Van Vugt, courtesy Glenbow Archives.

Methodist Mission, Morleyville in 1875.
From a sketch by Dr. Neavitt, NWMP.
Courtesy Public Archives of Alberta.

John Laurie. Courtesy Glenbow Archives.

The Real John Laurie

Yamnuska acquired its non-native name from the same person for whom John Laurie Boulevard in northwest Calgary is named. Laurie was born in Ontario in 1899. Educated as a lawyer and having served in World War I, he moved west in 1920 and taught high school in Calgary. The Stoneys became John Laurie's passion, and he spent a lot of time on the reserve, teaching for almost nothing and putting his legal training to use as an advocate for the tribe in its dealings with the federal government. He gathered historical information about the various Stoney families, took their pictures and recorded their music. Along with his dictionary of Nakoda words, all this material was given to the Glenbow Archives in Calgary.

Laurie's best-known contribution to Canada's First Nations was to help found the Alberta Indian Association, of which he became secretary in 1944. Made an honorary Stoney chief, Laurie died in 1959. Yamnuska was officially named Mount John Laurie in 1961, apparently at the request of the Stoneys themselves, who got the name amended to "Mount Laurie (Îyâmnathka)" in 1984.

The Yamnuska Area Today

There are two guest ranches, one large lodge and one youth camp currently operating in the Bow Valley below Yamnuska. Industry is here, too, and it continues to alter the landscape.

Brewster's Kananaskis Guest Ranch and the Rafter Six Ranch Resort still send dudes around the area on horseback each summer. The Kananaskis operation is now styled "Golf Resort" after a nine-hole course was added in 2001. The Rafter Six has been used as a location for several Hollywood movies and for many commercials.

In 1931 the Calgary YMCA opened Camp Chief Hector at Bowfort Lake—now Chief Hector Lake—on the Stoney reserve 5 km east of Yamnuska, where the Canmore YMCA had tented for a few years previously. In the years that followed, many a young camper made the trek to the summit of Yamnuska. Several notable Rockies climbers and guides were connected with the camp in the 1960s and 1970s, among them Dwayne Congdon, Billy Davidson, David Dornian, Jim Elzinga, Bruce Keller, John Lauchlan and Murray Toft. In 1972 the Stoney Band took over the camp for their own use, renaming it Nakoda Lodge and catering mainly to German tourists wanting an authentic aboriginal experience. After the main building burned, Nakoda Lodge was rebuilt and opened in 1981 as a facility primarily for conventions. Meanwhile, Camp Chief Hector had relocated south of the Bow River at Chilver Lake west of the reserve boundary, where it took over the Diamond Cross Guest Ranch buildings in 1972. The camp continues to operate today, with adventures on and around Yamnuska an integral part of its many programs.

Not far beyond Yamnuska's parking lot, Lafarge Canada quarries a particularly quartz-rich layer of sandstone (the Chungo Member of the Belly River Formation) that the company uses for making a certain type of cement. According to a spokesperson for

The original Camp Chief Hector on the east shore of Chief Hector Lake. Photo from the Camp Chief Hector 65th Reunion Memoirs.

Modern Nakoda Lodge on the same site as Camp Chief Hector. Yamnuska in the background. Photo Gillean Daffern.

"Before leaving the crest of the mountain, the quartet high-hatted the mountain goats with 'Don't sing Aloha when I go', and then the descent was made in safety with the aid of flashlights and flypaper." (From Camp Chief Hector newspaper "The Daily Pifle", describing a record-setting climb of the mountain in 1931.)

Top: The quarry below Yamnuska.
Bottom: The old dynamite storage shed near the quarry.
Photos Gillean Daffern.

Lafarge, the quarry dates to 1949. It is now about 200 x 200 m in size and not included in the surrounding protected area, much to the disappointment of those who wish the mining had not destroyed so much of the colorful, lichen-covered sandstone outcrop. The quarry will not be allowed to expand farther east, so the remaining cliff will be saved from industry. But it will not be protected from climbers, who continue to trample the vegetation. Clearly some remedial work is needed here.

In the late 1960s, American wildlife aficionados Kathy and Mickey Bailey started the Wildlife Unlimited game farm at the junction of Highway 1A and the Yamnuska access road. The intent was to provide captive wolves, cougars, bears and other beasts that could be photographed and filmed—

for a fee—in a natural-looking setting. However, by 1978 the business had failed and the Baileys had abandoned the operation. Members of the Stoney Band used the main building for a while, but today it's a ruin.

Yamnuska looks out over Bow Valley Provincial Park, which was created in 1959 to protect some of the more valuable wildland at the mountain front on the south side of the Bow River. Yamnuska, located on the north side, was not included. But in 1997, after environmentalists had lobbied the provincial government for many years—Diane and Mike McIvor of the Bow Valley Naturalists were especially persistent—a diamond-shaped patch of crown land about 4 x 7 km in size (1493 hectares) was set aside as the Yamnuska Natural Area.

Essential improvements were made in 1999 and 2000. A proper parking lot for climbers and hikers was built to replace the mud-hole that had passed for a parking area at the quarry gate. Public toilets, picnic tables and a bulletin board were installed. Volunteers from the Friends of Yamnuska, Bow Valley Naturalists, Friends of Kananaskis Country and Bow Valley Trailminders joined a crew of minimum-security prisoners to reroute the trunk trail up the mountain, which had begun at the quarry, to a new trailhead at the parking lot. Lafarge Canada helped to fund this work.

Also in 1999, the natural area grew by 81 ha along its southern edge. In 2002, the Yamnuska Natural Area and Bow Valley Provincial Park were consolidated into one protected area known as Bow Valley Wildland Provincial Park. It's important to keep in mind that only the south face of Yamnuska and the slopes below it are protected. The northern slope of the peak—meaning most of it—still has no protective designation. The next height of land to the north is the southern boundary of the new Don Getty Wildland Park. Perhaps the province will see fit to close the gap and thereby give all of Yamnuska better protection. This unique and wonderful little mountain certainly deserves it.

The Hard Stuff

How Yam Came to Be

Confronted with the notion that lofty Yamnuska was once part of the seabed, many a non-geologist has expressed surprise. When told that the mountain has been shoved many kilometres to the northeast, it's natural for these people to exclaim, "What?!" Usually they soon give up trying to understand.

Really, it's not all that complicated or mysterious. We now know that much of Western Canada once lay under the sea, and that the sedimentary layers deposited on the seabed were thrust up to become the Rockies. In the making of mountains, things get pushed around. That's basically it.

The details are fascinating. During the middle of the Cambrian Period half a billion years ago, the Yamnuska area was part of a wide, submerged continental shelf, something like today's Grand Banks of Newfoundland (again: in geology, the present is the key to the past). North America was moving generally eastward, relative to today's directions, and Alberta was out on the trailing edge, low-lying and thus covered by seawater. Not far west, the continental shelf dropped away into the great depths of the ocean. But the Yamnuska area was on the shelf, and the water was shallow. When Yam's beautiful limestone layers were being laid down about 525 million years ago, the water was very shallow indeed—at times less than 10 m deep, barely below the waves. Lots of living things swam there, scuttled across the seabed and burrowed in the oozy lime mud that hardened to become the Eldon Formation.

While fossils of any kind are quite rare in the Eldon's thick limestone layers, the strata are mottled with a lacy network of the mineral dolomite, which indicates that worms and other soft-bodied burrowing organisms ate their way through the sediment when it was still soft. The lack of other evidence of life suggests that (a) during this particular part of the Cambrian Period in this particular part of the world soft-bodied creatures had the seabed to themselves, and soft-bodied creatures are seldom preserved as fossils, or (b) there were hard-shelled organisms around, but they were so thoroughly decomposed that nothing remains of them— this is a good bet—or (c) the hard-shelled organisms chose to die elsewhere (as unlikely as it seems, this is a possibility because many sea animals migrate).

Whatever choice you prefer, bear in mind that while you're climbing on the south face of Yamnuska, two things are certain. One is that the rock you're gripping is made mostly of interlocking crystals of calcite, each originating within a tiny bacterial cell. So the rock has been made by living things. The second ultimate truth about the Eldon Formation is that every bit of it went through the guts of soft-bodied marine organisms, which is to say that you're climbing on worm poop.

Because the old western continental shelf was steadily sinking, a great deal of rock was deposited on top of the Eldon Formation. A lot of rock had already been deposited below the Eldon, because this subsidence had been going on for a long time. When you add all the layers below the Eldon and above the Eldon, the accumulated thickness of strata reached at least 10 km. That's what a billion years of riding around on the trailing edge of a continent will do.

But nothing lasts forever, and this lengthy quiet period in the geological history of western Canada came to an end about 175 million years ago. North America, which by this time had joined most of the world's other landmasses to form a supercontinent called Pangea, split away and began to move

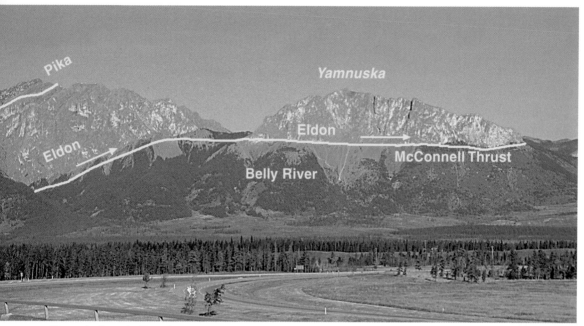

Yamnuska from the Trans-Canada Highway at the mountain front. Names of rock layers are shown, along with the thrust fault that underlies the mountain. Arrows indicate the direction the rock above the fault moved.
Photo Ben Gadd.

Ben Gadd pointing out the McConnell Thrust.
Photo Chic Scott.

northwestward. Western Canada was now on the leading edge of the continent, a place where violent geological events occur.

A plate collision is a violent event indeed, and that's what happened next. Our continent began heading northwest at about 10 cm per year. The adjoining floor of the Pacific Ocean continued to move northeast. Continental rock is lighter than ocean-floor rock, so North America began to slide over the Pacific seafloor, scraping off whatever material was deposited there and bulldozing it upward into a coastal mountain range like that of the Andes. Meanwhile, the leading edge of the oceanic plate was descending hundreds of kilometres into the earth below the continent, and it was melting down there. Magma was rising, burning its way up through the crust to emerge as powerful volcanoes of the type that explode. This was back in the days of the great Jurassic reptiles. No doubt the ridges were cleared of dinosaurs with each blast.

There was more. Landmasses the size of Vancouver Island were being carried northeastward on the ocean floor. When North America ran these landmasses down, they got ripped loose from their moorings and added to the west coast like log booms pushed ahead of a tugboat. Thus did much of western British Columbia join the Canadian confederation back in the Mesozoic.

Now recall that there was 10 km of sedimentary rock lying in neat layers on the old continental shelf. Caught in the squeeze between the advancing continent and the advancing landmasses, those layers found themselves pushed hard to the northeast. They wrinkled up like an accordion. Great folds began rising from the sea in echelons of ridges, each growing higher and higher as the rock bent and buckled under the strain. Earthquakes were frequent.

For a while the Yamnuska area lay east of the worst of this, beside a shallow inland sea that rippled where the prairies are now. As the new mountain ranges of western Canada grew, rivers carried eroded material into that sea. Geologists have looked carefully at the sediments deposited there, finding bits of the rising Rockies in them, recognizable grains that must have come only from certain layers. Fossils found among the redeposited particles have been used to date the deposits, and this combination has allowed science to establish the timing of mountain building across western Canada. As follows. The ranges rose from southwest to northeast, beginning about 175 million years ago, give or take 10 million years—what the heck, this is geological time—and ending about 45 million years ago. The Rockies around Lake Louise seem to have been above sea level and shedding sediment by 100 million years ago, perhaps earlier. The front ranges around Banff and Canmore were standing proud by 85 million years ago. The rock of Yamnuska was on the move soon thereafter.

By "on the move," we mean that literally. Along with the wrinkling of the landscape came thrust-faulting, a process that breaks large areas of bedrock loose and pushes them up and over the surface. Thus was Yamnuska's deeply buried Cambrian rock ramped upward and northeastward over layers higher in the sequence, coming to rest at least 13 km—maybe as far as 45 km—from

where it started, lying on Cretaceous shale (the Belly River Formation) 445 million years the younger.

One might think that finding old rock on top of younger rock would create quite a problem for government geologists George Dawson and Richard McConnell when they saw it in Yamnuska in 1884. But thrust-faulting had already been studied and explained in Europe, where it is common in the Alps. The Canadian scientists knew what they were looking at. In an 1886 report McConnell was clearly speaking of Yamnuska when he wrote, "The fault plane here is nearly horizontal." This feature is a classic of Canadian geology, and it's named for McConnell.

Important: the mountain we call Yamnuska was not pushed into position in its present form. Yamnuska is but a remnant of a much larger sheet of rock that moved. Erosion during and after mountain building has carved that huge, thick sheet into the mountains and valleys we see today.

Bear in mind, when you stand in the Bow Valley looking up at Yamnuska, that three or four kilometres of rock have been eroded from over your head in the last 75 million years. Bit by bit, all that rock has been carried eastward, first into the Cretaceous sea mentioned previously, later onto the prairies after the sea dried up, and more recently toward the location of Calgary by ice-age glaciers. These days the Bow River is the eventual recipient of whatever gravity tugs down from the heights on either side of the modern valley. The Bow River's load of sediment is supplied to the South Saskatchewan, which joins the North Saskatchewan east of Prince Albert to become the main Saskatchewan River, which dumps the sediment into Cedar Lake near The Pas, Manitoba. Given the amount of mixing along the way, if you grab a handful of mud from the Saskatchewan River's delta the odds are good that it will contain a tiny bit of Yamnuska.

Hans Gmoser climbing. Photo Philippe Delesalle.

2 The Early Climbs

Chic Scott

"I looked back along the base of Yamnuska. How many times had I been along here? How many times had all of us been out to climb old Yam? It was without a doubt the CMC's stomping ground, their playground. If only Yam could talk, what a tale it would tell—the countless epics; sweat, blood; the noisy passage of this boorish lot."
(Billy Davidson)

In the spring of 1952, twenty-year-old Hans Gmoser hitchhiked along what is today's 1A Highway from Calgary to Banff. Recently arrived from Austria, he was anxious to see the Rocky Mountains for the first time. As he approached the jagged line of peaks he noticed one in particular rising sheer above the highway: Yamnuska. "A silent and graceful silhouette, massive and yet so elegant. I was fascinated. A beautiful rock face took shape. In one straight line it rose to the sky. My eyes were fastened upon it and as the mountain stood there solemn in this May evening, a silent promise was made."

Above top: Yamnuska as Hans Gmoser would have seen it in 1952. Photo Chic Scott.
Below: Chic Scott. Photo Lloyd MacKay

31

The Fifties

Yamnuska is Discovered by Climbers

The practice cliff. Bob Hind instructing for the Calgary Section of the ACC, c. 1953. Photo Jim Tarrant

"It's still my favourite mountain after all these years." (Franz Dopf)

Although youngsters from Camp Chief Hector had been climbing up the back of Yamnuska for twenty years and the Calgary section of the Alpine Club of Canada (ACC) had been conducting rock schools on the sandstone crags near the road since the late 1940s, it seems that no one had ever considered climbing the south face.

Later that summer of 1952 Hans hiked to the base of the cliff with Marj Bugler, a nurse at Camp Chief Hector. As they ate lunch at the east end of the cliff, Hans had an opportunity to admire its dramatically steep profile. It was an intimidating sight, but also—for a climber—inspiring.

It wasn't until November 23 that Hans was able to keep his promise with Yamnuska. Early in the morning seven climbers drove west from Calgary along the old single-lane highway in one of the gas guzzling cars of the era. At the wheel was Walt Sparling, an active member of the local ACC section. As well as Gmoser there was Leo Grillmair, a friend of Hans' from Austria, John Manry, Isabel Spreat, Jean Hewitt and one other, still unidentified, named Roy. It was a beautiful, warm autumn day as they hiked up the slope to the cliff. There had been no snow yet that year and the wall above them was dry and inviting.

Hans had already been out climbing several times in his newly adopted country, but Leo had broken his leg the previous January and had been recovering for months. This was his first chance to get out and climb. Though his leg was weak, he had hands and wrists of steel from his trade as a plumber. Back home in Austria, Hans and Leo had been friends; in fact, they had come to Canada together but had never climbed together. Yamnuska would be their first opportunity to share a rope.

Leo was chomping at the bit when they arrived at the base and soon was scampering up the first cliff above the scree-covered ledges. Arriving at a secure spot, he decided he should tie in, so he hollered down to Hans to throw him up the end of the rope. He was joined by Isabel Spreat, an English physiotherapist. Since coming to Canada in 1950 she had been climbing at every opportunity and had already climbed with Hans earlier that summer on Mount Edith near Banff. Because she spoke some German she got along well with the Austrians.

They began working their way up an obvious line of cracks and corners that slants up the cliff just right of centre. Hans followed on a second rope with John and Jean, while Walt and Roy brought up the rear with a third rope. Before long it became apparent they were moving too slowly and that there was serious danger from falling stones. Hans soloed on ahead to rope up with Leo and Isabel while the others began to descend.

At about two thirds height the trio arrived at a pedestal at the base of a ten-metre vertical wall. This tricky step offers small square-cut holds overlooking tremendous exposure. It is not for the faint of heart. Leo made quick work of what is often considered the crux of the climb and scrambled over easy ledges to the base of a large chimney. As he belayed the others, he looked up and wondered if it would go; would the chimney lead to the top of the cliff or would it pinch off in unclimbable overhangs? It was late in the day and he did not like the thought of reversing the route. Also the sky had turned grey and it was beginning to snow. The situation was becoming serious. Deep inside the chimney, Leo squeezed between the two walls, sometimes climbing with back and knees and sometimes with feet against opposite walls. After bringing the others up to a safe ledge, he explored a cave-like recess above and was surprised to see light coming through a hole in the rock. Scrambling up, he poked his head out and pulled himself onto the windy top of Yamnuska. They were up!

With no pitons or carabiners and with only the most rudimentary of footwear the trio had succeeded on a climb that has frightened many heavily equipped climbers for decades. Although Isabel remembers wearing vibram-soled climbing boots, Leo

Hans Gmoser. Photo Philippe Delesalle.

Leo Grillmair. Courtesy Leo Grillmair collection.

wore only crepe-soled street shoes and Hans thinks he may have worn old leather ski boots. But they did have a nylon rope, a birthday gift that summer to Hans from Leo.

As the snow fell they coiled the rope and prepared to descend. There was no thought of the summit that day—they had climbed the south face of Yamnuska simply for the joy of climbing and had established in *Grillmair Chimneys* the first modern climb in Western Canada. Elated, they slithered down the back side of Yam, rounded the east end and bounded down the slopes to their car. By this time, Leo's shoes were much the worse for wear with holes worn through the soles from the rough rock.

Recently Isabel wondered why the south face of Yamnuska hadn't been climbed before, "because it is so near the road and has an easy way down the back when you've got to the top." She also commented that "The section [ACC] people probably thought we were nuts. When you're that age people are often surprised or shocked at what you get up to."

In late 1952 a third Austrian arrived in Canada. Franz Dopf had been Hans Gmoser's climbing partner back home in Austria. Enticed by tales of high wages and unclimbed mountains, Dopf joined Gmoser and Grillmair in Calgary.

On October 18, 1953, Dopf and Gmoser added a second route to Yamnuska. The *Calgary Route*, as they called it, followed a huge slanting gash left of the summit toward the west end. Gmoser and another Austrian, Kurt Lucas, had tried the route earlier, but had turned back when Lucas took a fall. The successful duo of Dopf and Gmoser found it harder than *Grillmair Chimneys* and placed several pitons on the climb for protection. The crux came right at the end, a strenuous squeeze chimney that still proves difficult for climbers today. After the climb Dopf and Gmoser crossed the summit and down-climbed *Grillmair Chimneys*—laughing and talking all the way, only a small slip away from eternity.

Isabel Spreat. Photo Isabel Spreat collection.

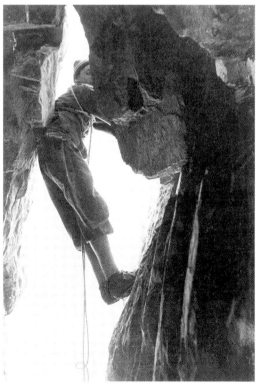

Franz Dopf on the first ascent of *Calgary Route*. Photo Hans Gmoser.

Opposite: P. Monod on the crux pitch of *Grillmair Chimneys*. Photo Don Vockeroth.

Franz Dopf. Photo Franz Dopf collection.

Right: Heinz Kahl.
Photo Glen Boles.

Below: Kurt Lucas, Hans Gmoser and Franz Dopf during
an early attempt on *Direttissima*. Photo Leo Grillmair.

The third route established on Yamnuska by these young men, and the finest, was named *Direttissima*. Inspired by the direct lines on the great walls of Europe's Dolomites, they wanted to create a route that would rise directly to the summit from the scree. The crux lead was low on the climb, the 2nd pitch in fact, a short, rounded crack capped by an overhang. Eventually Gmoser made wooden wedges and tied nylon loops through a hole drilled in the end. After driving these into the crack, he hung stirrups on the loops and climbed using direct aid. It was, indeed, a new type of climbing, one that had never been seen in Canada before. Several attempts were made by Gmoser, Grillmair, Dopf and Lucas before success was theirs.

Unfortunately, Dopf and Lucas were not along on the final successful climb. On September 14, 1957, Gmoser and Grillmair teamed up with newly-arrived German climber Heinz Kahl to complete the route. The prominent overhang near the top was almost a stopper, but Gmoser, leading out to the left, reached a line of cracks and chimneys that continued upward. In fact, Gmoser led almost the entire route until near the top where Kahl insisted he make his contribution and took over the lead. With legs bridged wide apart over 350 metres of air, Heinz climbed the final chimney to the summit crest.

Standing on the top in the wind, "Heinz lifted me right off my feet," Gmoser wrote, "and threw me over his shoulder in an outburst of joy. We were really lost for words and simply laughed and shook our heads. It had been so difficult and at times so frightening that now the feeling of relief and joy was simply overwhelming."

The ascent of *Direttissima* in 1957 marked the pinnacle of Gmoser's achievements on Yamnuska. A successful guiding career was now taking much of his time and he was also turning to the challenge of bigger objectives —Mount Alberta, Mount Logan and Mount McKinley. But for Brian Greenwood, who had just arrived from England in 1956, the love affair with Yamnuska was just beginning.

Hans Peter Trachsel on
Direttissima. Photo Urs Kallen.

Brian Greenwood. Photo Bugs McKeith.

Ron Thomson. Photo Ron Thomson collection

In 1957 Brian made his first statement on Yamnuska: *Belfry*, a short but difficult line toward the west end of the crag. He first attempted the climb with another Englishman, Dick Lofthouse, who led the overhanging 1st pitch. He returned later with Ron Thomson, a Manchester climber, and finished the route. Steep and intimidating (it now gets a 5.8 rating), it was climbed in a one-day push in impeccable British style, no pitons being placed and only natural protection being used throughout. Thomson soon moved to the USA, but Greenwood stayed and made Yamnuska his own for the next two decades.

During the 1950s few climbers disturbed the solitude of the ravens. It was a small group indeed who ventured up there on the weekends. There was no trail, no guidebook and little chance of a rescue if you got into trouble. If you wanted to buy a rope or a pair of boots there was a minimal selection available from Hector Elliott at his home in northwest Calgary. In those days there were no other developed crags and no sport climbs available, so if you wanted to go rock climbing you climbed on Yamnuska or went further west into the mountains and climbed to the summits of Mount Louis or Eisenhower Tower on Castle Mountain. For the few climbers who did hike up to Yamnuska, *Grillmair Chimneys* and *Calgary Route* were the popular choices. *Direttissima* was the pinnacle of rock climbing prowess in the Rockies at the time and was rarely climbed. Little known *Belfry Route* was feared by most and was climbed even less. During the 1960s all this would change.

> *"The more you went up, the more you saw of it, the more you became attached to it."*
> *(Brian Greenwood)*

The Sixties

Halcyon Years on Yamnuska

"The Mountain Club is like a biker gang. Once you're a member you can never not become a member." (Urs Kallen)

"The Calgary Mountain Club was pretty much the Hells Angels of the mountaineering world at the time… (Bruce Keller)

Perhaps the most important event of the decade came right at the start, on Wednesday, July 8, 1960, when the Calgary Mountain Club (CMC) held its first meeting. The stuffy Alpine Club of Canada didn't seem to be meeting the needs of the crowd of young climbers that was growing in Calgary. Moreover, the newly formed CMC was full of energy and ready to take on new and heroic challenges. Members came from around the world—Austria, Germany, Britain, Switzerland and New Zealand—and were joined by adventurous young Canadians. For the next 30 years, until the 1990s when the youthful energy finally settled in Canmore, the CMC would be the focus for new climbing developments in the Rockies. And Yamnuska would be their home cliff.

Early members of the CMC were young Germans and Austrians like Klaus Hahn, Dieter Raubach and Gunti Prinz. They lived together in what was probably Calgary's first climber's crash house, located near Memorial Drive at 735-1st Ave. NW. From all accounts they had a good time: lots of late

Klaus Hahn and Dieter Raubach.
Photo Klaus Hahn collection.

The 1961 accident. Left to right: Klaus Hahn, Les Mills, Dieter Raubach, Millie Arabski and the unnamed victim. Photo Klaus Hahn collection.

Carrying the victim to the car. Left to right: Dieter Raubach, Klaus Hahn, the victim and Les Mills. Photo Klaus Hahn collection.

night parties with plenty of alcohol and enthusiastic sing-songs.

In 1961 Hahn and Raubach had just started up *Grillmair Chimneys* when a distress call came up from below. Someone had been hurt and help was needed. So began an epic rescue, likely the first on Yamnuska, that entailed cutting down several trees near the base of the cliff to make a travois-like stretcher. It was a rough trip for the injured man as they dragged him down the scree, then carried him along game trails through the bush back to the car. It was then they decided to build a trail up to the base of the cliff. They spread the word through the CMC, hung some flagging along the proposed route and soon a rough trail began to take shape.

New route activity had been quiet for four years when in 1961 Brian Greenwood teamed up with Norwegian Jim Steen to climb his second route on Yamnuska—*Unnamed Route.* Following a diagonal slash at the west end of the cliff, it has over the years become a beginner's favourite. After the climb Greenwood and Steen likely stopped in the quarry at the base of the hill for a drink. In 1949, when Canada Cement had begun blasting for sandstone, the workers had tapped into a spring and now a stream of delicious cold water ran from the end of the pipe. For decades climbers would fill their bottles before heading up the hill or stop and refresh their parched throats at the end of a long day on the cliff.

Dick Lofthouse had returned to England to continue his studies in chemistry, but by 1962 he was back in Canada. The quiet climbing scene of the Fifties had been replaced by the energy of the Sixties and Dick was soon up on Yamnuska establishing new routes. Before he was finished he would have nine to his credit.

On May 27, 1962, Lofthouse and Greenwood climbed *Gollum Grooves* at the east end of the crag. Greenwood had recently discovered Tolkien's classic *The Lord of the Rings* and over the next decade would name several routes (and even his own children) after characters in the book.

Dick Lofthouse. Note helmet, belay gloves and homemade harness. Photo John Martin.

Jim Steen. Photo Glen Boles

Above: Hans Gmoser on *Red Shirt*.
Photo Urs Kallen collection.

Later that summer Lofthouse and Greenwood teamed up with Heinz Kahl to climb the quintessential Yamnuska classic—*Red Shirt*. Greenwood had attempted the route many times before, but on June 10, 1962, he discovered the key—the intricate traverse left at about mid-height—and they finished the climb that same day. The name comes from a tatty red shirt that Brian often wore and is rumoured to have hung high on the cliff so he could see from below exactly what point they had reached. Although the route has now acquired a 5.8 rating, it was for many years listed as merely 5.6. Brian in his article in the CAJ wrote, "The route while not technically difficult, is quite long and exposed. It will probably settle down to a standard grade IV [European Grade] compared to, say, III for the chimneys." Despite Brian's modest appraisal, it has scared the pants off climbers for years, has been the scene of a number of dramatic rescues and of one very tragic death. In fact, undergrading of routes on Yamnuska in the early days was simply a fact of life.

Below: Brian Greenwood's route description for *Red Shirt* from the CMC route log book.

Opposite: Heinz Kahl leading the last pitch on the first ascent of *Red Shirt*. Photo Gunti Prinz.

RED SHIRT - ROUTE on MT. YAMNASKA

JUNE 10, 1962

PARTY : BRIAN GREENWOOD, HEINZ KAHL, DICK LOFTHOUSE (FIRST ASSENT)

The RED-SHIRT-ROUTE marks the beginning of the second phase of exploration on MT. YAMNASKA. In the first phase the more obvious weaknesses were climbed and now, with one possible exception, all these obvious lines have yielded routes. In the second phase, it is the less obvious, and to some extent, artificial routes that will be climbed. This phase will probably bring a much larger number and variety of climbs throughout the length of the face due to the much closer examination of the face that will now be made.

The RED-SHIRT-ROUTE is marked on the face by the bowl, a hollow scoop some 300 yards east of the Grillmair Chimneys. The route itself begins at the bottom left hand corner of the bowl and follows a line tending left for approximately the first half of the face. Then a long traverse to the left is followed by a sweep back to the right with the end of the route just to the left of the top of the bowl. The route, while not technically difficult, is quite long and exposed. It will probably settle down to a standard grade IV compared to III for the Grillmair Chimneys.

"We all lived so simple. We took a sleeping bag along and slept under the open stars." (Lilo Schmid)

Lilo Schmid. Photo Inge Stolz.

Ed Peyer on *Chockstone Corner*. Photo Urs Kallen

By this time Brian Greenwood had begun importing climbing gear from around the world and selling it from his Calgary home, located in the prestigious Elbow Park district not far from the Glencoe Club. For two decades Brian's home would be a focal point for the climbing community and often would rock late into the night with loud parties. Brian had little time for gardening, so much to the consternation of his neighbours the hedge grew out of control, the lawn went uncut and the paint peeled from the house. Meanwhile, from his basement he offered the Calgary climbing community the best gear the climbing world had to offer—Charlet ice axes, Himasport down gear and Galibier boots from France, and from California the hottest new item on the market: Chouinard chromoly pitons. To purchase this gear, however, it was necessary to negotiate the giant white Hungarian Kuvasz dogs, Mithrandir and Saruman, who guarded the front door. If you were young and had climbing on the brain, the greatest honour was to be invited to tea with Brian and to be allowed to peruse his excellent library of climbing books.

In 1963 Dick Lofthouse and Heinz Kahl notched up another new route—*Chockstone Corner*. It had been attempted once before by Greenwood and Kahl, who had got quite high. Then Kahl returned with Lofthouse and knocked it off. Dick acknowledged that Heinz had led the entire climb. In describing the crux pitch (a chimney that narrows into a bulging crack), Lofthouse said that "[Heinz] worked some rocks around in the back of the crack till he could get a sling round, then stand in the sling." Today the pitch goes free at 5.8 and can be well protected with camming devices. That same year Brian Greenwood continued his harvest with *A Route*, climbed with CMC regular Gordon Crocker.

One of the most notable achievements of the summer came on September 7, when rising star Don Vockeroth led Lilo Schmid, a young German girl, up *Direttissima*—the first ascent by a woman. Lilo was an athletic gymnast and made short work of the route despite the huge, full-shank boots that she wore. Lilo recently recalled that "Don was, for us girls, our hero." When Don asked her if she would like to climb *Direttissima* "I felt so honoured I almost couldn't believe it. That whole night I couldn't sleep I was so excited."

Dick Lofthouse. Photo Chic Scott

Another important event of the year was the establishment of a Mountain Rescue Committee by CMC members. On October 31, 1963, the organization was officially registered under the Societies Act as the Calgary Mountain Rescue Group (CMRG), the chief aim being to provide a mountain rescue service for climbers outside the national parks and in particular on Yamnuska. Although many individuals played a leading role in the group over the years, no one contributed more than Dick Lofthouse. He was the first president and served the group in some capacity during its entire existence of almost 20 years.

Dick Lofthouse and Gordon Crocker on mountain rescue practice. Photo Inge Stolz.

CMRG practice. Lowering from the pedestal below the crux pitch on *Grillmair Chimneys*. Photo Inge Stolz.

Betty King and Lilo Schmid. Photo Inge Stolz.

Betty King. Photo Inge Stolz.

In 1964 Don Vockeroth exploded onto the scene with incredible energy. Don had first hiked up the back side of Yam in 1959 and had fallen in love with the mountain. During the first few years of the Sixties he had climbed all the classics, some many times. By the mid-Sixties he was ready to put his own stamp on the cliff. Recently he confided, "It was passion, passion, passion. I would set aside my work, I would set aside my social life, I would set aside anything because when I was out there I was in my medium. That's where I felt really comfortable. Everything was at peace… I was in love with Yamnuska. There was 4 or 5 years there that any opportunity I had I would be up there. It kept pulling me, I never could stay away."

On May 31 he and Greenwood climbed *Missionary's Crack*, a slightly ribald and erroneous reference to John Laurie who was actually a teacher and secretary of the Indian Association of Alberta. They had attempted the route three weeks earlier and had managed three pitches. On their second try they reached the crux of the climb, an overhanging, flaring jam crack with great exposure. Brian tried it several times but could not master the moves. Don then had a go but was also stopped. He came down, rested for a while, then went back at it, his only protection a sling around a rock wedged in the crack. After several strenuous layback moves he found a tiny finger hold on the left, just inside the flaring crack. Pulling hard on this, he smeared his foot on the wall to the left, then reached high right to a perfect jug handle. Don recalled it as a pitch that took strength. (Standing 6' 2" and weighing only 150 pounds at the time, he had a great strength-to-weight ratio.) Brian followed him up the crack, cursing all the way, but would not take a tight rope. Later that year, when Don and Lloyd MacKay made the second ascent, the jug handle at the crux pulled off. Lloyd took a whipper, but went back up and finished the pitch. It has been substantially more difficult ever since and now gets a 5.9 rating.

Self portrait of Don Vockeroth.

On June 2 of that year Don led Betty King, a young Canadian physiotherapist and member of the CMC, up *King's Chimney*, a route of modest difficulty at the west end of the cliff. Don loved to take folks out climbing. Recently he explained, "Because I had this love affair with Yamnuska I was dragging people up there all the time. And as soon as people realised that I was willing to take them out—they asked." This attitude eventually led to a remarkable career as a mountain guide.

On June 30 Yamnuska experienced its first fatal climbing accident. Brian Llewellyn Andreason, age 18, a recent graduate of Crescent Heights High School in Calgary and an active member of the Canadian Youth Hostel Association, had arranged to meet several friends at the base of Yam to do a climb. It appears he did not wait for his friends to arrive and started up *Unnamed Route* alone. When his friends arrived they found his body at the base of the cliff, Andreason likely having popped out of the first awkward chimney.

"Every time you climbed up to the base...we would sit down and just think about it. Think about the things that we did, think about where you were in the world and how great things in life were." (Don Vockeroth)

Forbidden Corner. Photo Don Vockeroth.

On October 12 and 13 Vockeroth and Lloyd MacKay, a lawyer originally from Nova Scotia, put up what may be the classic 5.8 route on the cliff (a route that Greenwood had already attempted). The two were as different as chalk and cheese: Don was tall, thin, laid back and climbed with the grace of a cat, while Lloyd was a short firecracker, bursting with energy and optimism. A year previously they had climbed about six pitches up the initial corner. At Thanksgiving, 1964, the pair returned. On their feet they wore stiff, heavy, Galibier mountaineering boots.

As Lloyd had a new bivy sac he wanted to try out, they decided to start the climb late in the day and bivouac. Arriving at the base of the cliff at 11 am, Don realised he had forgotten his water bottle and that it was going to be a dry, thirsty climb. At 6 pm they stopped for the night at the top of the prominent corner that splits the lower half of the face. The climbing to that point had been excellent—small holds and solid rock. Don recalled how they were running out about 12 metres between points of protection.

The bivouac was uncomfortable: they were thirsty and on the sloping ledge they kept sliding to the bottom of the bivy sack. When the sun finally rose, they drank the last of their water and were on their way again. The route-finding was intricate, but Don had examined the face from below and knew the landmarks. Don led the first crux, pulling over an overhang onto a thin, 80 degree slab and up to a pillar where he established a belay. Then Lloyd led the next crux, stepping out onto a vertical wall with tiny holds. There was little in the way of protection on these pitches, as only pitons were available in those days and no one would dare place a bolt. By midday they were on top, where they ran into a group of boy scouts who gave them a much-welcome drink of water. They named their masterpiece *Verboten Corner*, but somehow the name never stuck and today it is called *Forbidden Corner* ("Verboten" in English).

Lloyd MacKay. Photo Ron Langevin.

Within a week Don was renewing his attempts on a steep line to the right of *Red Shirt* known as *The Bowl*. When Don had tried this route with Brian in 1963, Brian had dislocated his shoulder and they had been forced to retreat. On October 18, 1964, Don and a fearless young Austrian woman named Inge Steinbach (now Inge Stolz) managed to push the route higher. Placing slings around 2x4s driven into the crack for protection, they climbed to the crux: an overhang at the top of a corner. Feeling that climbing the overhang direct would be too difficult, Don played on the wall to the right for hours. He went up and down several times, memorizing the moves. Only a few metres from easier ground, he figured he had it worked out. He came down, rested, then set out on the wall. When he reached the high point he "went to make the moves. I reached and I didn't have it. It wasn't there. So I PUT MY HANDS ON MY HIPS. Then the wall started moving... the wall moved away from me but it still didn't register and I was still thinking of how to do the crux. Then it registered. I was falling off. So I reached, but I missed it." Don fell about 12 metres and they called it quits for the day.

Don Vockeroth during an early attempt on *The Bowl*.
Photo Inge Stolz.

Don and Inge returned on October 25 for another attempt. This time they tried a new approach: the direct line up the corner and around the overhang. And it went surprisingly easily. There was a bold layback under the overhang, then a move around into a flaring corner. A nice little foothold about the size of a thumbnail helped him work his way around the edge of the overhang while he changed hands. Above this they cruised the next two pitches to a small corner just a stone's throw from the top. Don set out on the last pitch, reached an overhang and hesitated. It was a loose block and he just didn't want to trust it. He felt a fall here would have serious consequences. It was almost dark and he was tired. So once more they retreated from their vertical world via four long rappels. Don recalled, "We went down in the dark. That was scary. No bolt kits. I had the only flashlight. I came down, [the] flashlight in my teeth."

Inge Stolz. Photo Inge Stolz collection.

Two other routes established that summer were *C Route* by Brian Greenwood and Walter Schrauth, and a completely new finish to *Chockstone Corner* called *Bottleneck* by Dick Lofthouse and Al Cole. Recently Urs Kallen commented that it was a fine effort on the part of Lofthouse, who did all the leading, and is perhaps harder than the 5.8 grading that it gets.

Al Cole on the east end of Yamnuska. Photo Glen Boles.

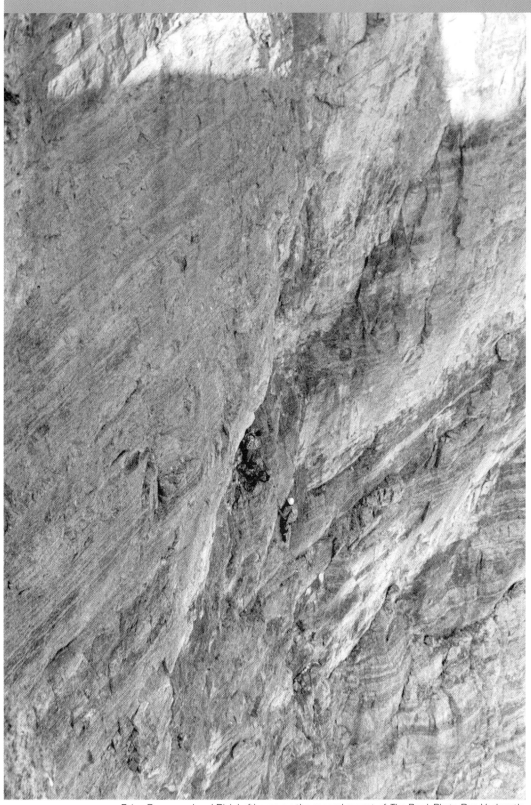

Brian Greenwood and Dick Lofthouse on the second ascent of *The Bowl*. Photo Don Vockeroth.

Spring came early to Yamnuska in 1965. On May 29 Vockeroth and MacKay returned to *The Bowl* and quickly climbed to the high point. Then Lloyd led the last pitch. Hitting the loose overhanging block with his hammer he felt it was sufficiently solid and climbed it. For Don it has always been a bit of a disappointment that Inge didn't share in the honour of the first ascent. He recently commented: "Inge was so stoic. She had a lot of talent and she never panicked."

Don added a second route that year. *Pangolin* (named for a type of scaly anteater found in southeast Asia), was really an idea of Greenwood and Lofthouse who invited Don to come along with them. Vockeroth remembers the route as "very sustained, very hard." He said this was perhaps because the route was not his conception. "There's a different psyche when it's your climb. You're actually preparing yourself for leading. When it's not your climb you're sort of hanging back and saying 'Hmmm! That looks hard.'"

The three each took a turn at leading a pitch and near the top of the route arrived at a cave below a steep, overhanging chimney crack. It looked very hard and unprotected to start, so Greenwood got creative and put two carabiners on the end of a rope and repeatedly threw them upwards toward a v-slot about six metres above. Eventually they jammed and Brian proceeded to prussik the rope to the high point, then free climbed above that to the top. Don followed the pitch and was surprised to find it wasn't as hard as it had looked, but was spectacularly exposed.

Two other new climbs were added that summer of 1965. Vockeroth again teamed up with Greenwood to create a new, two-pitch start to Lofthouse's *Bottleneck,* and Greenwood and Lofthouse teamed up to climb another short east-end route that is now called *B Route*.

Don Vockeroth on the first ascent of *Pangolin*. Photo Dick Lofthouse

In the late summer of 1966, Swiss climber Urs Kallen arrived in Calgary. Only a few weeks later, on September 21, Klaus Hahn took him out to Yamnuska, where they made the first ascent of *The Toe*. It was the beginning of Urs' life long love affair with the cliff and the first of many new routes he was involved in. Perhaps afterwards Klaus and Urs visited the Exshaw Legion for a beer. Klaus recently remembered, "You finished climbing, and unless you were in a hurry to get home, you would go those few miles west and go to the Legion—especially on a Saturday."

In the spring of 1967 Yamnuska lost one of her most devoted admirers when Heinz Kahl died of leukemia at only 33 years of age. He had established three classic routes on the cliff: *Direttissima*, *Red Shirt* and *Chockstone Corner*. Always friendly and happy, he was greatly loved by everyone. Brian Greenwood remembered Heinz as "one of the greatest people. His enthusiasm was tremendous."

"I still look forward to all those great new lines that I see. And I wonder who is going to do them and I point them out to Andy and I point them out to other people ...

"Yamnuska is so interesting. It depends on the light that you see it in. All of a sudden you see lines that you only see in certain light." (Urs Kallen)

Urs Kallen and Billy Davidson.
Photo Urs Kallen collection.

Hans Fuhrer. Photo Bill Browne.

That year Vockeroth continued to mine new routes including *Corkscrew*, so named because it twisted its way up the cliff. The original idea had been to climb a series of corners just right of what is now referred to as *Yellow Edge*, but the climbers—various combinations of Vockeroth, Greenwood and MacKay—got drawn out right onto easier ground. On one occasion, after a frightening traverse with little protection at about half-height, a blank overhanging wall was encountered. Here MacKay eventually placed eight expansion bolts but ran out of bolts before easier ground was reached, so they retreated.

Finally, on September 7 Don returned with Greenwood and Swiss-born Hans Fuhrer, with whom Don worked at the Columbia Icefield, providing information and doing mountain-safety work for Parks Canada. Climbing back up to their high point, Greenwood placed a final bolt and an aid pin that took him onto free-climbing ground above. By this time it was getting late in the day, so when Vockeroth reached Greenwood above the bolts he suggested Brian bring up Hans while he ran out the rope beyond. He wanted to get up before the last light faded. The rock was superb and Don was in top form, perhaps "bolder than I should have been." But he added, "When you're climbing that well and you focus really hard things start to get easier." So in the pale twilight, with no belay, Don basically soloed the last two pitches to the summit.

"The rock was superb and Don was in top form, perhaps 'bolder than I should have been.'"

Opposite: Brian Greenwood and Hans Fuhrer on the first ascent of *Corkscrew*. Photo Don Vockeroth.

The historic image of Brian Greenwood on *Super Direttissima*. Photo Urs Kallen.

Brian Greenwood on *Forbidden Corner*.
Photo Urs Kallen.

The following spring Greenwood and Kallen hiked up to Yamnuska in deep snow and stood below the highest point, gazing up at the overhangs searching for a new route. Their idea was to climb what they called at the time *Super Direttissima*. While new snow fell, Greenwood led the first steep pitch and Kallen, a first-rate photographer, captured this historic image with his camera. It would take four years and many tries, but eventually the route would be climbed. (See page 74.)

In the autumn of 1968 Vockeroth added his eighth route to Yamnuska. As expected, he had explored the route previously with Greenwood. This time he was partnered with Charlie Locke, a young Calgary climber who was making a name for himself in winter climbing, ski mountaineering and on the north faces. The pair had almost got to the top with perhaps one pitch to go when time ran out and they decided to retreat. On the way down the rappel rope got stuck and while they struggled to pull it free it grew dark on them. Unexpectedly, they were committed to a long, autumn bivouac. Don recalled, "We were fools. I had a long-sleeved shirt, Charlie had a T-shirt. We both sat on a tiny little knob. I was sitting in the back, Charlie in the front. Charlie was freezing to death so we switched positions. And then it started getting cool, and then it started to rain a light little rain, then it turned to snow. We shivered all night."

At first light they wrestled the rope free and continued the descent. Arriving back in Banff, Don went home to his rooming house run by Iva Lindow, known to all as Mum Lindow. No one was around that early in the morning, so he just went to his room. About noon Mum Lindow poked her head in Don's room and was shocked to see him there, in bed. Everyone had been extremely worried and a rescue was being organized. No doubt Don felt a little sheepish about it all and apologized profusely.

A week later Don and Charlie went back and finished the route. In honour of Mum Lindow, who had worried all night about her boys, they named it *Mum's Tears*.

Charlie Locke and Brian Greenwood in the old parking area. Photo Don Vockeroth.

John Martin. Photo John Martin collection.

That same autumn yet another young Calgary climber began to put his stamp on Yamnuska. John Martin had been climbing on Yam since 1964, repeating many of the classics. Then in just one month he created three new routes. On October 6 with Stu Slymon, also a young Calgary native, he climbed *Easy Street*. On October 20 he added *Windy Slabs* with Slymon and Martin Bowen, a Welsh climber who was part of the CMC scene for a few years. Finally, on October 26 Martin and Bowen added *The Tongue Right Side* which John now refers to as "an undistinguished climb."

"You stand at the bottom and you look up and it towers over you and there's all that loose rock." (John Martin)

Stu Slymon on *Red Shirt*. Photo John Martin.

Windy Slabs. John Martin leading 1st pitch, Martin Bowen at base. Photo John Martin collection.

58

The view from *Easy Street*. Photo John Martin collection.

Mountain rescue hut below the cliff.
Photo Klaus Hahn.

"It's very hard to have climbing that's just a weekend activity, and that was even more true then. Just because the stakes were high. It drove off anybody who didn't have some fairly intense desire to do it. You didn't have to climb very long to realize how quickly you could be dead." (John Martin)

At Halloween that year of '68 a group of free-spirited Calgary climbers left their mark on Yamnuska in a very different way. Ron Robinson, Graham Law, Pam Fahrner and Val Hess climbed *Unnamed Route* while their friend Jane Peterson hiked around the west end, carrying up plastic bags full of bright orange and green paint. Then, just below the top, on a smooth overhanging wall off to the left of the climb, they painted a pumpkin about a metre and a half in diameter. In 2003 it was visible even from the bottom of the cliff (repainted, perhaps?), and had folks wondering where it came from. Now you know.

Besides the pumpkin painting, another unique event took place in 1968: the Calgary Mountain Rescue Group built a fibreglass-roofed rescue hut below the east end of the cliff. Klaus Hahn spent several days levelling a platform, then other CMRG members carried up the hut materials and assembled it in just one weekend. It was not meant to accommodate climbers; it was meant to be a storage hut for rescue equipment like the large, awkward stretcher that was sometimes used. Unfortunately the hut didn't last long. The next winter a huge piece of ice peeled off the cliff and scored a direct hit.

On April 13, 1969, John Martin and Stu Slymon intended to climb *Bottleneck*, but after climbing much of the route they rapped off. The next day John returned with Yamnuska veteran Dick Lofthouse to finish the route and to collect the hardware he had left during the retreat the day before. Without incident they climbed high on the wall. Then, as John was leading the second to last pitch, "My technique failed me. It may have been that I pulled something off that was loose. I just fell off.

"All of a sudden I was airborne. I went shooting down through space, and bang I hit a ledge really hard. Saw stars. Came shooting out into the sunlight. I was tumbling but not particularly fast, and I remember two things specifically: I remember thinking what a nice day it was, and I remember realizing that I had knocked a lens out of my glasses and being annoyed about that.

"I had a couple of soft-steel angle pitons in, which I thought were quite good. When the pull came on the rope they came out but I didn't know that. The time dilation was such that I thought I had fallen to the end of the rope and pulled Dick off and we were both going to the bottom. So it was quite surprising when all of a sudden I stopped falling."

John estimates he had fallen about sixty metres. Apart from a broken right kneecap, a separated shoulder and a broken bone in his foot, he was amazingly unhurt. He had not been wearing a harness as was customary at the time; the rope had simply been tied about his waist in a bowline on a coil. He had been wearing a helmet and this likely saved his life when he hit his head on a ledge. He called up to Dick but received no response. Dick had been slammed into the rock by the force of the fall and been knocked unconscious. Someone far below on the scree had witnessed the fall and was hollering up, "Do you need a rescue?" John responded in the affirmative and the figure ran off to summon help.

Dick came to and began a rescue operation. There could have been no one better for the job. He was the leading member of the CMRG and well-trained in rescue technique. John recently recalled that Dick was "Absolutely fantastic. There was probably no one else around who would have known what to do, or been equipped to do it." Dick would lower John two rope lengths at a time then rappel down to him. By the time they reached the scree the rescue team had just started to arrive. John recalled, "The first guy there was Brian Greenwood. He knew I smoked and the first thing he said was 'Are you OK?' And the second thing was 'You lost your smokes, and he handed me a smoke. I saw the Brian Greenwood that people who climbed with Brian saw, which was the person who was completely serious, completely competent."

Brian would be involved in another rescue later that year. On Sunday, November 9, a climber fell and hurt himself near the top of *Red Shirt*. At about 10 pm Brian climbed down in the dark with food, water and sleeping bags for the stranded climbers and then spent the night with the party, who I am sure were greatly comforted by his presence. In the morning he brought them to the top of the cliff—just one of many rescues that the CMRG performed over the years on Yamnuska.

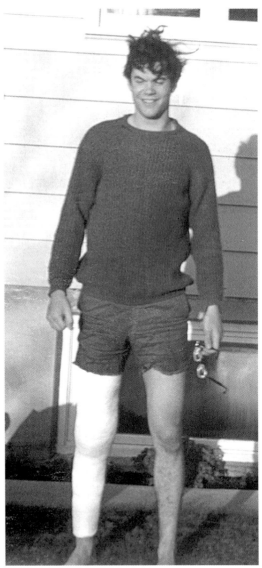

John Martin in cast after the accident on *Bottleneck*.
Photo John Martin collection.

John Moss. Photo Urs Kallen

Bill Rennie in the slot on *Balrog*. Photo Andy Genereux.

In 1969 Brian made his most notable statement on the south face of Yamnuska. With British ex-pat climbers John Moss and Nat Nicholas he climbed *Balrog*. It was a line he had attempted many times before, but he had always been stopped about two thirds of the way up by a very difficult lead up and left into the final bowl. Eventually the technical crux yielded, but bolts were required for aid. However, the climb wasn't over yet. Andy Genereux, who did an early free ascent of the route, recalled that "the upper pitches of *Balrog* are virtually without protection and the climbing is sustained 5.8 for four or five pitches. I think it's the mental crux of the route."

In keeping with years of tradition, Brian named the route for the great beast in the mithral vein of Khazad-dum in *The Lord of the Rings*. Recently John Martin commented that "Brian was really persistent on *Balrog*. I guess it was the project that took him the longest. Certainly it was a big step ahead in terms of technical difficulty. It was probably the hardest route on Yam for at least ten years after that." In his characteristically modest fashion, Brian recalled that he "just happened to be there at the right time." The truth of the matter is that he was a talented and determined climber.

Perhaps the most bizarre incident in the entire history of Yamnuska happened this last year of the decade. On September 7, Eckhard Grassman (No. 1 Swissman) attempted to drive his Land Rover up the steep hillside to the base of the cliff. Now Eckhard was not an entirely normal fellow: legend has it he could drink a full glass of beer while standing on his head. He was a math professor at the University of Calgary and he loved winter alpinism. He had been a member of the team that had climbed the great north face of the Dent d'Herens in the Swiss Alps in the winter of 1963. On this climb he had been lucky to escape with his life and had sacrificed pretty well all his toes to the savage god of winter climbing.

Nat Nicholas on *Direttissima* while Stu Slymon belays. Photo John Martin.

Eckhard Grassman. Photo Urs Kallen

With Eckhard on this fateful day were Urs Kallen (No. 2 Swissman) and George Homer (the Englishman). Billy Davidson later wrote in the CMC newsletter how they lifted high the cable that blocked the road and "drove to the top of the quarry, with the Englishman thinking 'that saved us a little walk,' and he prepared to get out. But the Little Red Jeep did not want to stop there, he wanted to go climbing with his three friends. Pointing his nose at the cliff, he proceeded to smash his way up the overhanging hillside. No. 2 Swissman and the Englishman were a little frightened at the actions of the jeep, but No. 1 Swissman actually seemed to be enjoying it and at times seemed to spur the little jeep on. Eventually though, the jeep seemed to tire and stopped. No. 2 Swissman and the Englishman prussiked up the door handles and got out onto the grass. No. 1 Swissman stayed in and encouraged the little jeep to take a rest until they came back."

George Homer and Eckhard Grassman abandoning the Land Rover. Photo Urs Kallen.

The three of them hiked the rest of the way up the hillside and proceeded to climb *Forbidden Corner*, likely the third ascent of the route. Ten hours later they were back at the Land Rover.

"No. 1 Swissman sat in the front seat again and gave encouraging kicks to the jeep until his nose was pointing downhill. He then stopped and No. 1 Swissman stepped out. Now none of the three friends really knows what happened, but No. 2 Swissman said later that he thought it was the kicks that made the Little Red Jeep angry. For suddenly he started to roll down the hill. Now No. 1 Swissman tried to step back, but only managed to get one foot inside and as the jeep gathered speed, he hopped alongside until the speed was too great; he then withdrew his leg. The three friends stood and watched as the jeep in its naughtiness hurtled down the hillside all alone and entered the bush. Here the outcome of his anger was terrible to behold. Not a tree or bush stood in his way until his anger was spent. He then leaned on a tree and came to rest."

Eckhard, Urs and George rushed down the hill and found the Land Rover "still breathing." Eckhard was not finished yet and again attempted to head up the hill, but "the jeep refused silently but firmly, so the three friends had to persuade him to push over the tree he was leaning on and go down."

Back at the road, the jeep decided it had had enough for the day and refused to run. "So No. 2 Swissman was delegated to hitch-hike home, get a car and drive back. He did this, doing minor car repairs on the way, and two hours later he arrived back and towed the naughty jeep and the two friends back home, for it was way past their bedtime. Good night!"

Looking back, the Sixties were halcyon days on Yamnuska. Twenty new routes were added to the cliff, many of them destined to become classics. Recently Brian Greenwood commented, "There never seemed to be any urgency to do a route. If you didn't do it this week, it would still be there next week, or next year." New routes were often undergraded. In John Martin's opinion, "The biggest fear was that you would overgrade a route and somebody would come along after you and say 'Well, it's not that hard.'"

Often a climber would run into other climbers in the parking lot or along the base of the cliff and likely as not they would know one another. Most were members of the Calgary Mountain Club. There were no guidebooks, so if one wanted to repeat a route one had to go to a CMC meeting, either to talk to someone who had done it or to read the first route description in the club's big book.

There was almost no instruction in those days, so climbers learned by trial and error high on Yamnuska. One had to accept serious risk even to climb at a modest level. Protection was poor, pitons being all that was available. In the words of John Martin, "How often did you have that sensation; you're out there leading and you realized that if you fall off here you're probably going to rip the belay out and you're both going to the bottom. Or worse yet, you're belaying and you know perfectly well that if he falls off you're both going to the bottom."

Equipment was still pretty rudimentary. Climbers often just tied in about the waist, although some were designing homemade harnesses. There were few rock shoes available, so big boots were normal and it was only toward the end of the decade that climbers started to use helmets. Piton hammers were often just stuffed in the back pocket of the knickers that most climbers wore.

Despite all this, the standard of climbing on Yamnuska was incredibly high. It may be that routes like *Missionary's Crack*, *Forbidden Corner* and *The Bowl* were amongst the hardest climbs in North America at the time. They certainly were among the most frightening. And the skills learned on Yamnuska were soon being applied to larger alpine climbs: Mount Temple north face, Howse Peak northeast buttress and the east face of Mount Babel.

The Seventies & Early Eighties

Blank Walls and the British Invasion

"You can climb on vertical stuff and overhanging stuff at 5.8. You can finesse your way through pitch after pitch of really beautiful situations where you're just sharing it with the swallows." (Tim Auger)

On May 23, 1970, Brian Greenwood and Urs Kallen climbed *Smeagol*, Brian's last new route on Yamnuska. The month before, as if to wrap up his career on the crag, he and Kallen had published the first climber's guide to Yamnuska, a small book of only two dozen pages. Offering pitch-by-pitch route descriptions, it was the first modern climber's guide in the Canadian Rocky Mountains. Almost half the routes in the book had been put up by Brian.

Brian had a tremendous influence on the development of Yamnuska. Over a period of 13 years he had pioneered 11 new routes and many others that he had started and had never finished. In fact, when he was asked in 1997 if there were any unfinished projects, he replied, "Yes. Most of them."

Lofthouse was still very active that summer and had found a new partner in Scotsman Dick Howe, a long-time member of the CMC. The pair had their set ways of doing things. Howe always led the odd-numbered pitches and Lofthouse the even-numbered. As well, they always climbed on a Saturday as Lofthouse liked to spend his Sun-

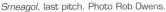

Smeagol, last pitch. Photo Rob Owens.

days at home. In 1970 the two Dicks teamed up to establish a pair of fine new routes: *Dicks' Route* and *Dickel.* The former was climbed in retaliation, Howe says, for the theft of *Smeagol* earlier in the year by Greenwood and Kallen. Both three-pitch lines were climbed in traditional style: no pitons were used, only homemade nuts and natural protection.

There was another bold climb done that summer of 1970. Inspired by the great solo climb of Walter Bonatti on the southwest pillar of the Dru, Don Gardner, a twenty-one-year-old climber from Calgary, made what was perhaps the first solo ascent of a difficult route on Yamnuska: *Red Shirt.* At the beginning he actually belayed himself with a rope, but "It got so ponderous, up and down, feeding out rope. It was making me scared." So he coiled up the rope and just free-soloed. Having climbed the route many times before, he was familiar with the moves and was amazed at "the ease at which it went and the lack of fear." On the last pitch he pulled out the rope again and gave himself an auto belay on the awkward traverse to the top. He said he had an eye on soloing *Direttissima* someday but never got around to it. That honour would go a few years later to another CMC legend, Andy Genereux.

"It's a nice feeling to know that you have contributed a little bit to the climbing history of Yamnuska." (Dick Howe)

Top: Dick Howe. Photo Bugs McKeith.
Bottom: Don Gardner. Photo Tim Auger.

Ian Heys (left) and Jeff Horne. Photo Jeff Horne collection.

Top left: George Homer. Photo CMC collection.
Left: George Homer below Forbidden Corner.
Photo Urs Kallen.

Bugs McKeith at his one-person tea party on top
of Yamnuska. Photo Bugs McKeith collection.

The 1970s saw the arrival of perhaps a dozen outstanding British climbers in Calgary. Greenwood and Lofthouse had, of course, been around since the Fifties. Dick Howe had arrived in 1963 and Jon Jones in 1967. Some of the new arrivals like Nat Nicholas, John Moss and Ian Heys later returned home. But others like George Homer, Jeff Horne, Jack Firth, Bugs McKeith, Rob Wood, Chris Perry and Trevor Jones stayed and had a huge influence on the development of Canadian climbing. John Martin recently commented, "There was a tradition of technically good climbers in England, so they learned to climb among climbers who were good, whereas there wasn't a tradition of strong technical climbers here at all." These British climbers also brought with them some of the newest developments in climbing equipment: commercial nuts, EBs and the Whillans harness.

That summer of 1970 saw three of these Brits make contributions to Yamnuska: Homer and Heys climbed a direct-direct start to *Bottleneck,* and Horne and Heys did the first free ascent of *Pangolin.* Urs Kallen recently recalled that "Heys was probably the best of all those guys. In a different league."

Jon Jones. Photo CMC collection.

The 1971 climbing season began with what is, perhaps, the most tragic chapter in the history of Yamnuska. Late in the afternoon of May 2, John Kula, 22 years of age, led out across the last pitch on *Red Shirt*. Tied into a single piton at the register box, John Martin (not the well-known author of sport-climbing guides mentioned previously), sat and belayed. Kula clipped into the two solid pins on the traverse, but when he reached the corner he climbed straight up rather than move around to the right. Realizing he was off route, he began to climb back down. Then he fell.

The force of the fall pulled the single piton at the belay and ripped Martin from his ledge. Both climbers found themselves hanging in space, suspended from the rope. Kula told Martin that a hold had come off and asked Martin to lower him a few metres to a ledge. But Martin succeeded only in lowering himself to a ledge. For some reason, even from the ledge, Martin could not lower Kula.

In the words of Ben Gadd who spoke to Martin 30 years later, "The rest must have happened very quickly. Kula was wearing a chest harness, perhaps loosely tied, over a slippery nylon shell. And he was skinny. Martin saw the harness creeping up and warned Kula. However, Kula was unresponsive. The pressure on his chest would have affected his breathing, and he might have been losing consciousness. He cried out once (Martin called it a 'cry of despair'), his arms rose, and he slipped out of his harness."

As Kula fell to his death on the scree below, Martin managed to retain his balance on the ledge. Then he climbed back up to the belay ledge and spent what must have been a terrible night, alone and frightened, having just witnessed such a frightful event. It wasn't until early afternoon of the following day that Banff National Park wardens John Wackerle and Keith Brady, flown in by helicopter to the top of the climb, were able to lower him a rope.

Archie Simpson Hut Book Entries
by Billy Davidson in 1974

Billy Davidson. Photo Urs Kallen.

ONE DAY
fTER 4c

With a knife so sharpe, it's edge
gleaming like silver, I cut the wood,
or should I say the meat from a dead
tree, if you arn't already aware, I'm cutting
a — NO — I'm carving a flute - To blow
my mind away in shapes of musical notes.
Now for all of you who have been
writing, it's Billy's Poem hour. (Bomr in
the Background)

— On my first day of Acid,
My ture love brought to me.
one straight jacket and a fresh supply
of LSD
— On my second day of Acid,
My true love brought to me.
A hit of meskelin, one straight jacket, and
a fresh supply of LSD.
— On my third day of Acid,
My true love brought to me.
30 fresh joints, A hit of meskelin, one straight
jacket, and a fresh supply of L.S.D.
— On my fouth day of Acid
My true love Brought

Blew my mind — The devil made
me do it! TA — TA tA — TA — TA — TATA

The Bolting Trilogy
(to be sung to "The railroad Trilogy" by Gordon
Lightfoot)

by William Lighthead

VERSE There was a time in this fair land
when bolting was not done.
When the tall blank walls stood
virgin in the sun.
Long before the Hardings and long
before the steel.
When the tall blank walls were
too silent to be real.

But time has no beginning and
histry has no bounds
And to these virid walls they came
from all around
They drilled apoon her blankness
And put the routes up tall.
Put up the ladders and belays
to the dismay of us all.

Chourse For they look into the future and
what did they see.
They saw a bolt ladder running
from the top to the scree.
Up blank walls to hanging belays.
Swinng their (blankets) hammer and
drawing dismay

Look away said Robbins
Across these mightey walls
To Tis-sa-ack
I only used 110 in all
I only used 110 in all —

Behind the blue Rockies
the sun is declining
The stars they are shinng
At the break of the day
Across the wide walls the
climbers lay stoned
In their hamocks
In a land far away.

Oh we are the bolters
who work apoon the walls
swinning are hammers in the
bright blazing sun
Living on tuna and drinking
bad water
Putting in bolts
till the long day is dowe

Hut entries courtesy CMC collection.

Right: Archie Simpson.
Photo Urs Kallen.

Right: Archie Simpson.
Photo Urs Kallen.

Meanwhile, in the valley behind Yamnuska CMC climbers finally got a home. Led by Archie Simpson, another British ex-pat, club members resurrected the rotting remains of an old loggers' cabin. A new wooden floor was built, aluminum printing plates provided by Urs Kallen were attached to the roof, and an airtight stove was installed. For much of the Seventies this cabin would be a home away from home for one-of-a-kind characters like Billy Davidson and rising stars like John Lauchlan, who would spend many cosy nights here with their friends, telling stories and enjoying the intoxicants of their choice. During the day they would hike back up the hill and around the east end of Yam to climb a route, or more likely they would explore the climbing potential of what would come to be called CMC Valley.

Before and after. The old loggers' cabin in CMC Valley (right) and the Archie Simpson Hut in the early 1970s (below). Photos CMC collection.

71

Despite the bad start, 1971 eventually turned out to be an excellent year for new routes. Don Vockeroth finally succeeded in climbing a route he had been working on for years: *Kahl Wall*, which he named after his friend Heinz Kahl. The name is also a play on words, as "kahl" means "bald" or "bare" in German. Don had attempted the route at least half a dozen times before with partners like Lloyd MacKay, John Moss and Charlie Locke, and had got to within about three pitches of the top. He had already climbed the crux pitch, a blank wall at mid-height, with a mixture of aid and free climbing that included three bolts. Then on July 1 he returned with Tim Auger, a fine climber from Vancouver who later would become the backbone of the Banff National Park mountain rescue team. From the high point Tim led up an arching corner, then stepped out right onto a blank wall. Tim remembers the exposure as breathtaking, but the solid rock and a couple of small ledges invited him to keep going. A hexentric nut inserted sideways into a shallow water runnel was all the protection he had for much of the way. Finally he placed a bolt and finished the pitch. Don led one more pitch, then Tim ran it out to the top. *Kahl Wall* is now considered one of the classics, the crux pitch going free at 5.10a. Recently Don explained that he "never thought it was going to be an aid route or have any aid on it at all. I just wasn't up to doing it free." Trevor Jones recently referred to it as the first of the modern climbs on Yamnuska, the first that ventured out onto the blank walls.

Kahl Wall was Don's last new route on Yamnuska. For eight years he had had a passionate affair with the mountain, but soon he would move west to Rossland, leaving his beloved cliff behind. Don was the first homegrown Canadian climber to be truly on the leading edge of the sport. He had an exceptional ability to focus and recently revealed that "when I was climbing really intensely it would trigger something in my mind and I would start hearing different music... Beethoven. It's the power of the mind. If you could just keep that intensity you could achieve so much."

Tim Auger. Photo Neil Bennett.

"In the Rockies, when you're climbing somewhere else, when you're on the north face of Alberta or on the east face of Babel, you're always comparing it to Yamnuska... First you climb the ice, then you climb Yamnuska, then you put your crampons on and you climb some more ice and you're on top." (Tim Auger)

Opposite: Tim Auger on crux pitch of *Kahl Wall*. Photo Tim Auger collection.

Jon Jones. Photo CMC collection.

Opposite: Jon Jones on the first ascent of
Necromancer. Photo Jon Jones collection.

The wave of new British climbers continued to make a statement. On July 4 Jeff Horne teamed up with Billy Davidson to climb *Freak Out*. The modern guidebook calls the climb "loose and strenuous … an adventure climb in the finest Yam tradition." In Andy Genereux's opinion, "For its era it's probably the most sustained and technically demanding climb on the shittiest rock on the mountain, and I for one was impressed." At the other end of the cliff, Jon Jones and George Homer climbed *Necromancer* (meaning wizard or magician). They had seen the "good line" the previous year after getting off route while attempting *Mum's Tears* with John Martin and Billy Davidson.

That summer, old hands Dick Lofthouse and Dick Howe teamed up to climb *Shuftee*, a four-pitch variation finish to *Direttissima*. Recently Howe explained the name: "It's a British word, let's have a shuftee at this or a look at something." It was Lofthouse's last new line on Yamnuska. For close to twenty years he had explored the cliff and had contributed nine routes. At times a prickly person to be around, he was praised by all as a steady and safe climber. It was also Howe's last new line. "I'm thrilled that I actually managed to do three new routes. It's a nice feeling to know that you have contributed a little bit to the climbing history of Yamnuska."

In 1972 the *Super Direttissima* that Urs Kallen and Brian Greenwood had tentatively explored back in 1968 was finally climbed. Over the years the name had changed and the route was now called *CMC Wall*, partly to honour the Calgary Mountain Club and partly because the locals wanted their own "wall" just like Yosemite's El Capitan. In 1969 and '70 Urs, Brian and Billy Davidson had made numerous forays onto the overhanging route. In August of 1970 Urs returned to Switzerland for 20 months. While he was away Billy ventured alone onto *CMC Wall* several times, but more importantly he mastered the art of aid climbing, in 1970 climbing North America Wall on El Capitan, in 1971 climbing Iron Suspender on Wakonda Buttress and the north face of Gibraltar Mountain—all serious aid climbs.

"Billy Davidson was the Charlie Porter of the North. They both were loners and they both pushed aid climbing to new standards. They were in a league different from the rest of us." (Urs Kallen)

On the morning of June 3, Kallen and Davidson hiked up the hill to the base of Yamnuska. Lagging far behind were Greenwood and Tim Auger. Urs and Billy jumared the 1st pitch, then looked fearfully up at the frayed rope hanging down from the overhang above. Eventually Urs made the commitment, attached his jumar to the rope and swung out into space. In the words of Kallen, it "was the psychological lead of that day. By the time I got to the stance I was just finished." When Billy arrived on the ledge beside Urs they exchanged words with Brian far below and decided to go for it alone. They dropped the fixed ropes to the ground and turned their attention to the wall above.

Billy led the 3rd pitch to the high point of earlier attempts and there they bivied. The next morning Urs led a moderate 4th pitch, mixed aid and free, to a good ledge. Then the climbing got hard. The 5th pitch was the infamous A4 traverse where Billy had to resort to stacked pins in horizontal seams. As the pitch rose to a high point then descended, it was psychologically even harder to follow and Urs feared that a mistake would unzip the entire pitch and result in a giant pendulum. It was getting late in the day, their bolt drills were all broken, and they were nearing their psychological limits. They hollered down to Greenwood to climb to the top and drop them a rope. But Urs recalled that Brian said, "'Nah. You guys are all right.' We couldn't believe it that he

left. So Billy with his ingenuity fixed one of the bolt kits and got us going again." Pushing on, Billy was caught by dark, so they drilled some bolts and spent a miserable night hanging in slings. At one point a bolt pulled, completely freaking them out.

In the morning they were determined to get off that day. For hours Urs drilled on the 7th pitch, placing four rivets, then a bolt, then repeating the sequence again and again. After placing 22 bolts and rivets and becoming seriously dehydrated, Urs backed off with about five metres to go and let Billy finish the lead. The 8th and 9th pitches went more quickly, a mix of aid and free climbing, then they were on top. Urs recalled, "We were glad it was over."

Davidson wrote later, "I feel happy then suddenly lonely. I somehow feel very isolated amongst all this rugged beauty. The sun, now just dipping below the mountains to the west, sends out lines of gold threaded with orange and purple hues. God, this is beautiful—should have a camera. No! This wouldn't look any different from any other sunset on film. Even the memory will fade in time. We climb for the moment, and the special enjoyment gained from that moment. Looking back and remembering will never be the same as the original experience. If it were, we should just sit by the fire for the rest of our lives; sipping beer, smoking and just remembering. Instead we climb on and on, searching out those most precious moments, wherever they may be found."

Laden like mules with ropes and iron, they came down the back side. By the time they reached the spring in the quarry it was dark. Vowing never to climb again, they left the gear and walked along Highway 1X to the service station on the Trans-Canada Highway where they curled up and tried to sleep for a few hours. When it got light they stuck out their thumbs and luck was with them—they got a ride that took them right to their front doors in Calgary. Urs had a quick shower and rushed off to work, where his fellow employees must have wondered what he had been up to.

Billy Davidson cleans *CMC Wall* 4th pitch. Photo Urs Kallen.

"When we got to the top, I was transfixed. The great height seemed to have me spell- bound. Right from then I knew I would be doing more climb- ing." (Billy Davidson at age 12 after hiking up the back side of Yamnuska with a group of boys from Camp Chief Hector)

Billy Davidson begins the A4 traverse on *CMC Wall*. Photo Urs Kallen.

"I think it's wonderful how the Canadians took to climbing." (Franz Dopf)

John Lauchlan. Photo Urs Kallen

While Kallen and Davidson were hanging from pins and bolts high above the scree, a new figure was emerging on the Canadian climbing scene: John Lauchlan, who would eventually become a cult figure even in his own lifetime. Like all Calgary climbers he cut his teeth on Yamnuska and must have felt compelled to make a contribution to the development of the cliff. Sometime in 1973 he teamed up with British hard men Al Burgess and Pete Thexton to make the first free ascent of *The Bowl*. However, his main project that year was the second ascent of *CMC Wall*, which was acquiring a big reputation. His partner was Jim Elzinga, who, like John, had just graduated from high school. On the first day they climbed one pitch, fixed a rope, then descended and spent a comfortable night at the CMC hut. On day two they climbed above the overhangs and bivouacked in hammocks. Then things started to go wrong. Early on day three, while leading the 4th pitch, Elzinga took a fall and dislocated his knee. Retreat over the huge overhangs was out of the question, so they decided to push on. The climb became epic. Jim was in severe pain, but trying to ignore it. The day was hot, and they had run out of water. And they were terrified by popping rivets. As John was leading the final pitch, someone leaned over the top and offered a rope. Safely belayed, John climbed the last few metres to the top and brought up Jim. But they still had to get down. Burning with thirst and exhausted, the pair descended the back side, Jim on his hands and knees, then slid down the scree slopes to the spring in the quarry where they could finally slake their thirst. The second ascent of *CMC Wall* had been just as memorable as the first!

Opposite top: Urs Kallen on the 2nd pitch during the first ascent of *Yellow Edge*. Photo Urs Kallen collection.

Opposite bottom: Davidson and Kallen descending following the first ascent of *Yellow Edge*. Photo Urs Kallen.

By 1974 both Urs and Billy were back on Yamnuska looking for more bold new lines. The Calgary Mountain Club was focused on Yosemite and into aid climbing at that time and felt that Yamnuska was an ideal cliff on which to perfect their technique. On May 4 the pair climbed to the base of the Yellow Edge, a prominent prow right of the Bowl. This time they were confident in their abilities and the climb—*Yellow Edge*— went like clockwork. Billy led the 1st pitch, which went free at 5.9, then Urs led the wildly overhanging and strenuous 2nd pitch. Billy led the 3rd pitch to the bottom of a corner where they bivied in hammocks. The next day Billy led the 4th pitch up the corner, then Urs led the 5th out right, using a mix of free climbing and tied-off knife blades. On reaching a good ledge he spent the night there, while Billy remained below on his ledge. On the final day Billy climbed up to Urs and led on to the top. The climb had gone smoothly and without epics. In Urs' words, "We were seasoned pros."

Brian Greenwood and Billy Davidson in the cave below *Grillmair Chimneys*. Photo Jon Jones.

Bruce Keller. Photo Trevor Jones.

Two days later John Martin returned to *Bottleneck,* where he had taken his incredible tumble five years earlier. While Jim Tanner belayed, he climbed the offending pitch. After a brief flashback at the crux, he made the moves and left the past behind.

On August 16 Brian Greenwood turned 40 and retired from climbing. The next year Billy Davidson also retired and moved west to Vancouver Island, where he has since followed his passion for kayaking and living off the land. Kallen remembers Billy as the quintessential aid climber. "He could get totally immersed in the problem at hand, could spend hours figuring out how to stack pins." In his opinion, Billy had mastered the sport of climbing and had simply become bored.

Two years passed with no new routes, then in 1976 John Lauchlan and another Calgary local, Bruce Keller, climbed *Dazed and Confused*, a loose and difficult climb at the west end of the crag. Keller recalled, "There was one section that both of us went up and down. It had about eleven or twelve pieces in thirty feet and none of them looked good, and then we had to do an aid move off a stopper that was only half jammed in. But we figured that we'd zipper the whole works and it wouldn't be a bad fall."

About this time John Lauchlan began a career as a mountain guide. Working through the Calgary YMCA, he and others inaugurated a program of climbing instruction which they named the Yamnuska Mountain School. Eventually it would grow into Yamnuska Inc., Canada's largest mountain-guiding service.

"5.9 was fairly easy to climb in Yosemite and totally awe-inspiring to climb in the Rockies." (Bruce Keller)

1976 saw a most unusual mountain rescue on Yamnuska. About noon on May 31, helicopter pilot Jim Davies landed a national parks mountain rescue team at the top of *Calgary Route*. Their objective was two stranded climbers who had spent the night on the cliff about 40 metres below the top. But there was a problem: in the scree there was nowhere to anchor the winch apparatus. A unique solution was found—they simply tied everything off to the landing gear of the helicopter. Tim Auger, who was sent down twice on the cable to bring the pair up, remembered thinking at the time that "As long as it didn't pull the helicopter down *Calgary Route*, we'd be OK."

On a sad note, the Rockies climbing community lost one of its leading lights in 1976 when Lloyd MacKay died of cancer. He had pioneered several classic lines on Yamnuska and had done much of the early exploration of Banff-area crags. Don Vockeroth recently summed up Lloyd in three words: "Talent, brains and vision."

By the middle of the Seventies Yamnuska was fading from the forefront of Rockies climbing. Great new climbs were being created on the other cliffs of the Bow Valley: on Ha Ling Peak (then called Chinaman's), Goat, Kid Goat and Nanny Goat Buttresses, Crag X and Heart Slabs. The many crags of CMC Valley were being worked out, and the Ghost River Area, that Yosemite of the north, was in the process of discovery. Yamnuska had seemingly been worked out; the classic lines mined. In 1977, as if to wrap up the era, Urs Kallen came out with a new edition of *A Climbers Guide to Yamnuska*. There were now 34 routes on the cliff and to some it was beginning to look crowded. It is interesting to note that routes were still being undergraded through the 1970s. Urs recently commented, "The whole problem with our generation was—5.7 was hard, 5.8 was harder and 5.9 was the limit. We never even dreamed of grading anything 5.9+ or 5.10. Even if we did climb that well, the grade that we would give it would be 5.9 and more than likely we would call it 5.8 because if you call it 5.9 it would be a bit of a testy thing in the

The 1976 rescue on *Calgary Route*.
Photo Parks Canada.

Calgary Mountain Club." Tim Auger has a slightly different explanation: "5.9 was supposed to be as hard as one could conceive, so if it was really hard you called it 5.8 because you left room for someone else."

The last few years of the Seventies and the first years of the Eighties were largely uneventful. However, during this time many young Calgary climbers learned to climb on the cliff. One of these was Andy Genereux, who would go on to become one of the most prolific rock climbers in the Rockies. In 1978, at the age of nineteen, he felt sufficiently confident to solo seven routes in a day. He started up *Unnamed*, then down-climbed *Calgary Route*. Next he soloed *Direttissima*—a tremendous achievement for one so young—and down-climbed *Grillmair Chimneys*. Walking east, he climbed *B Route*, then scrambled around the east end of the cliff and all along the trail at the base to climb *Windy Slabs* at the west end. He finished his remarkable day by down-climbing *King's Chimney* to recover a piece of gear that had been left on the route earlier in the day by one of his friends.

That same year of 1978 saw the end of an era: Greenwood sold his Elbow Park house. In May the entire climbing community gathered for one last party at the Greenwood mansion, then Brian moved west, first to Golden, then a few years later to Duncan on Vancouver Island.

Several new climbs were established during the late Seventies and early Eighties, but nothing of a seminal nature. In 1978 John Martin and Lynda Howard climbed *Gray Goose*, a line between *King's Chimney* and *Unnamed*. John explained recently how, "It's always fun to go out on a new piece of rock that nobody's been on before, and it's a project that you've been looking at, and it works first time." That same year Quebecois climbers René Boiselle and J. P. Cadot freed *Shuftee*.

Albi Sole. Photo Rob Rohn.

"We lost our beer, but we lived."
(Albi Sole)

Lynda Howard. Photo John Martin.

CMC barbecue in the mid-1980s. Photo Chic Scott.

In 1980, new British arrival Albi Sole and Canadian Greg Spohr attempted the line of corners to the right of *Yellow Edge*, the line that had been the goal of the *Corkscrew* team years earlier. Caught by dark near the top, Sole and Spohr retreated. Their ropes got hung up on the descent and they had to leave them to hurry down the hill to the CMC's barbecue in the meadows. Unfortunately, they arrived just as the last of the beer was pumped from the keg. The next morning they went back up to collect their ropes. During the night the nylon had been chewed on by rats, and it was with beating hearts that they jumared back up, only to find that the sling they had rappelled off in the dark had become untied and only the friction of the half-tied knot had held it together. Sole remarked years later, "We lost our beer, but we lived." The next summer Sole returned with Dave Morgan and finished the route. As they were both in the process of tying the knot, they named the route *Marriage Rites*.

Dave Morgan. Photo Dave Morgan collection.

Murray Toft. Photo Glen Boles,

Martin White. Photo Chris Perry.

Two other new routes were put up in 1981: *False Promise* by Alan Derbyshire and Murray Toft, and *High Voltage* by Chris Perry and Martin White. On the former, a short route at the west end of the cliff, the pair attempted the prominent large roof but were forced off to the left. Al Derbyshire confessed recently that "it was beyond our modest abilities." The latter route, Chris Perry admitted, did not receive its name because of the electrifying climbing involved, but because it zigzagged its way up the cliff like a bolt of lightening. In reality, Perry was unwilling to venture onto the blank walls and place bolts, so he followed the natural breaks where he could place traditional protection instead.

In 1983 Hans Gmoser, Franz Dopf and Leo Grillmair returned to Yamnuska for a historic reunion and with Ferdl Taxbock climbed *Grillmair Chimneys*. It had been over thirty years since they had pioneered the first climbs on the wall. At the time it seemed as though the glory days of Yamnuska had come to an end, but in every end there is a new beginning, and at that very moment a climbing revolution was building that would sweep Yamnuska into the next century.

> "It seemed as though the glory days of Yamnuska had come to an end, but in every end there is a new beginning."

Opposite: The 30th anniversary climb of *Grillmair Chimneys* in 1983. Top left: Leo Grillmair. Top right: Hans Gmoser. Bottom: Hans Gmoser, Franz Dopf and Leo Grillmair after the climb. Photos Ferdl Taxbock.

3 A Place in the Pantheon

Dave Dornian

The 1970s had come and gone on Yamnuska without the great strides and standard-setting events of the prior decade. The cliff had progressed from enigma to landmark to proving ground to training facility, and by the end of the Seventies, from a climber's point of view, it had become as much of a local hangout for Calgary climbers as a place for alpinists to cut their teeth.

New blood continued to flow along the veins and arteries of the old routes, however, pulsing with the beat of the mountain's heart. Young Calgarians, reared almost within sight of the crag and introduced to rock climbing through service groups like the Boy Scouts and the YMCA, worked their way through the list of classics identified by Urs Kallen and Brian Greenwood in their original guidebooks. These tantalizing pamphlets charted the ambitions of many a daydreaming schoolboy. Youths like Barry Blanchard and his friend Kevin Doyle, Jeff Marshall, Brian Wallace, and Bill Stark began returning again and again, pushing at the rock that would gradually begin to turn over and roll and gather momentum into the Eighties.

Above: Dave Dornian. Photo Gillean Daffern.
Opposite: Raphael Slawinski on the 6th pitch of *Highlander*. Photo Keith Carter.

The Eighties

The Only Climbing Number Worth Anything

"The only climbing number worth anything." (Barry Blanchard after climbing all the routes in Urs Kallen's 'Seventies guidebook.)

Barry Blanchard. Photo Chic Scott.

Just recently, alpinist Barry Blanchard, following on decades of achievement in the great ranges of the world, acknowledged the unique pride and sense of accomplishment attached to climbing on Yamnuska when, after more than twenty years of return visits, he finally succeeded in climbing all the lines described in Kallen's Seventies guidebook.

"7 summits, all 14 eight-thousanders, plebeian endeavours at best. Everyone, and I expect soon someone's dog, is doing them. 'To do' lists hardly worth the serious climber's consideration, doubly so if you're a serious Albertan climber. Take heed y'all, the gauntlet clangeth about your feet! On June 22 of this year I, Barry Blanchard, and in the company of my swearing bride I might add, ascended the mighty *B Route* on Yamnuska. With this success I entered into an ultimately elite pride of uberclimbers (to the best of my knowledge Andy Genereux is the only other to achieve this superhuman tick).

"ALL 34!

" Yes, you've read that right, no need to shake your head again. I've climbed all of the hallowed 34 routes described in Urs Kallen's 1977 masterpiece 'A Climber's Guide to Yamnuska'. The proudest, most manly climbing guide ever published, and the first guidebook I bought way back then… in my starry eyed youth.

"Cringe! Cower! Covet! Take up the torch all you lessers, for the true climbing challenge has been bellowed from the sacred summit of the world's greatest peak (Yam).

"7 continents, 14 high peaks, bah! CHILDSPLAY! I say, CHILDSPLAY! Not worth the gleaming sweat off my big hairy butt!

"34, that's what it's all about, friend. Get out there and start counting."

Despite his light-spirited preening in the paragraphs above, Barry Blanchard is not overeager to make claims for any grandiose achievements on the rock of Yamnuska. Although he was in the vanguard of the new wave of climbing that began to emerge on the cliff in the early 1980s, he maintains that the events that might be celebrated today didn't seem particularly significant at the time. Acknowledging their influence, however, Blanchard admits that Yamnuska was "massively important to me." As a young man growing up and learning to climb, he suggests that the mountain did more for him than he ever did for the mountain.

Beginning his explorations in the front ranges west of Calgary as a teenager, Blanchard went up to Yamnuska with boyhood partner Ron Humble "...pretty much directly after Wasootch"—an introductory area popular with beginners and teaching groups.

"I learned to climb up there on Yam— and I learned to route-find on rock. I remember being on *Belfry*, sitting while I was on belay and my partner was frigging around overhead, and I looked over at a little pinnacle, and realized that every feature mentioned in the guidebook didn't have to be, like, detached and 200 feet high. It was a bit of a revelation."

The young Blanchard was keen, going out every weekend, and then he managed to free up time and began climbing midweek, too. This led him to hook up with the young Jeff Marshall, "usually on Wednesdays." Memory can be a fragile thing after twenty years of high-altitude wear and tear. Jeff Marshall says today, of the same set of circumstances, "Blanch would call me up whenever he had a project where he didn't want [Kevin] Doyle to steal all the hard leads!"

However they found each other, Blanchard goes on, "Jeff was in his 'Junior' phase—we used to call him 'Dr. Risk.' We actually bought him a Beanie when we were in The Valley [Yosemite] in '81.

"Anyway, we had all the aid climbing gear, I think, when we went up on *Necromancer* that year, but when we got to the artificial climbing section we looked up and saw the pin scars and said '...you could put your hand there, and there...'

It seemed a natural thing to do. In the end it just went.

"I've always been a little disappointed that after *Necromancer* and *Kahl Wall* [with Kevin Doyle, in 1981] I didn't get the free ascent of *Balrog*, too. I was up on it and figured the climbing out, but had to hang on one of the bolts."

Blanchard had planned to return to *Balrog* in a matter of days, eager to do the first completely free ascent. But during the interval, unknowingly, Brian Gross and Dave Cheesmond went on the route with the same idea. A strong party originally from South Africa, and new to the region, they succeeded on the climb. This first free ascent is also variously attributed to Andy Genereux and Brian Wallace, whereas the guidebook *Bow Valley Rock* places Tim Friesen in the company of Cheesmond for the FFA in 1982.

The finer points of who freed what in those distant days, and when exactly they did it, is open to question. Blanchard suspects that the likes of the controversial Peter Charkiw may have sent *Necromancer* and perhaps also *Kahl Wall* free in earlier times and never been given credit for the achievement. Though there were not that many climbers on the cutting edge two decades ago, the scene was quite fiercely partisan. News travelled slowly between groups, and the different cliques were not always accepting of each other's claims.

> *"I've always been a little disappointed that after Necromancer and Kahl Wall...I didn't get the free ascent of Balrog, too."*
> *(Barry Blanchard)*

Bill Stark. Photo John Martin.

Brian Wallace. Photo Steve DeMaio.

Bill Stark & Brian Wallace Free CMC Wall

Bill Stark was twenty-three years old at the time of the watershed ascent marking the end of the third decade of climbing on Yamnuska.

Stark had begun his outdoor education at the age of 12 with the Boy Scouts, and later with the scrambling and hiking programs of the hostelling association in Calgary. It was through this latter group that he fell in with the notorious Calgary Mountain Club and began to climb in earnest through the 1970s. He remembers doing *Red Shirt* on Yamnuska in 1974, and being along on an early ascent of the groundbreaking waterfall ice climb of *Louise Falls* in '75.

"In the late Seventies Roger Neilson had an ad up on the wall of the Mountain Equipment Co-op, looking for partners. Together we did the first free ascent of *Dicks' Route*, thinking it was *Smeagol* (hey, we were young, and getting going). Then the second time out with Roger, we got lost on *Quasar* and put up *EEOR's Tail* [on the east end of Mount Rundle]. The third time up on Rundle, Roger is following and pulls off a ledge and breaks his leg."

Bill Stark had known Brian Wallace since the two boys were eight years old. They travelled to Yosemite together at the height of the valley's golden age of free climbing in 1977. There, the boys were much impressed, and were inspired to bring the "hard and free" ethos back to the home crags. Stark was unusual in the Bow Valley climbing community, being one of the first to embrace hard training, soloing and practicing indoors during the off-season on artificial walls. By contrast, Brian Wallace was a savant—a climbing talent bred from a background in gymnastics and a stubborn psychology that refused to take "no" for an answer. Stark describes how, on the route *Mean Mistreater*, under the massive roofs at the west end of Yamnuska, Wallace would take repeated falls, and get back on and fall off, and get back on, trying to free the moves—never considering artificial aids, or quitting.

Brian had been out with Jeff Marshall in the early Eighties and the pair had made the third ascent of *CMC Wall* together. Stark had also been on the route before, in 1979 with Mike Sawyer as well as with Wallace in 1980. Wallace asked Stark if he would be interested in going along for an attempt to free the route. This was not an invitation to be taken lightly. *CMC Wall* had gained in reputation, if anything, in the years since the first, multi-attempt ascent. Rumours of terrifying improvised hardware and the supposed impossibility of retreat from high on the route combined to keep casual suitors away.

On the day that he and Wallace went up to "just have a look" in early 1984, the weather was fine and winds were calm—good omens according to Stark. They carried "a basic Rockies rack, plus pins, Friends, and a hand drill."

Bill got the lead on the 2nd pitch, and it went better than anticipated. He freed it easily; a stretch of climbing that the received wisdom of the day said probably wouldn't go. While rearranging themselves at the stance, Wallace's shifting weight sheared one of the old belay bolts from the rock. The pair calmly replaced it and Wallace took the 3rd pitch. Bill gave directions from below.

And it went! They had been on the route for only two hours.

The 4th pitch fell free to Stark almost as easily. From the stance at the top of each pitch, to hear Bill tell the story today, the boys would hang from an arm and pump their fists overhead, celebrating the effort and cheering their success.

5th pitch. Bill checked the crack, then moved back to the slab. "I made the mistake of watching a pin fall, and seeing it vanish toward the scree without touching a thing!

"We collected a ton of gear from the Lauchlan/Elzinga epic (the bad-luck second ascent of the route), so that was great, too—

"I always believed in free climbing. Trusted it more. Why swing around on a shitty placement when you can put four points, stable, on the rock?" (Bill Stark)

Bill Stark. Photo Sharon Parker collection.

"Brian Wallace had a pathological lack of fear." (John Martin)

like a reward." Indeed, the two never hammered a new pin on the entire climb.

"At the top we were whooping and shouting. We'd done it! One day! Not only the first free ascent, but the first one-day ascent, too! Amazing! A guy we talked to in the quarry after we'd got back down, later, had heard us yelling and thought maybe we were in trouble or something, we'd been making so much noise. He was the only confirmation we had, the only person we'd seen all day."

Of the aftermath, and what it meant for climbing on Yamnuska, Stark says, "Of course this was cool, but I didn't think it was any really big deal in the larger scheme of things. Then Urs started saying at the Cecil [the Cecil Hotel in Calgary was host to the gossipy CMC club nights on Wednesday evenings], 'it's a whole new era, it's a whole new era!'"

Discussing the elements that led up to the opening of the new era on Yam, Stark opines, "We were influenced in the valley by the likes of Ron Kauk and Eric Weinstein, you see. There were always Canadians in Yosemite. On our first visit there we'd got up three elevens [5.11 pitches] and we'd come back to Alberta looking for cracks. We found everything back home under-graded."

In the years following their landmark climb, Stark backed away from the blooming Yamnuska free-climbing scene of the Eighties. He was attending school in Los Angeles, getting education and training prior to assuming a career as a professional diver. "I dropped out for a while, then Brian called me up again—he came to me with a picture of Suicide Wall. The route that would soon become *Astro Yam*." But Stark's life would keep him away from Yamnuska for the next decade, at least as far as adding new routes to the cliff was concerned. "In later years I went back to *Yellow Edge* with Al Dunham. I parapented off the top of Yam once..."

The 1984 Parachute Jumper

Located next to a major transportation corridor, convenient for everyone's fantasies, Yamnuska has never been the sole province of mountain people. With its broader appeal, the cliff has served often as a focus for passersby, and occasionally the interests of these people cross those of the climbers who frequent the area. Such was the case in 1984 when a BASE jumper miscalculated his trajectory from the summit of the peak and was snagged by his parachute on the lower reaches of the wall.

Tim Auger, called straight from home, was on the rescue with Lloyd Gallagher who had already climbed up to the injured subject with Rod Jager. The victim had jumped from the top, about 100 metres west of the finish of *Direttissima*. The wall was close to vertical where his chute hung him up, hooked on the rock.

He was dangling in a vertical position from his harness. Not on any established route, Tim had to climb up a couple of pitches to reach the site of the accident. "I'll tell you, all I could do was get up beside him—it was STEEP!"

They put pitons in a crack about a metre above the victim's head and tied the man in, in case the parachute released. The rescuers then built an anchor with pitons and perhaps a bolt, set up a pulley system from this, and with the addition of a second rope, Lloyd controlled the lowering from below. The victim was semiconscious and hurting. Tim thought he might have had a broken pelvis. Lloyd lowered the two of them together after Tim cut the victim free from the parachute lines and ducked underneath to piggyback the man around obstacles. At the ledge with Lloyd they rested, built another anchor and Lloyd lowered them the rest of the way to the bottom where a stretcher was waiting. A helicopter slung Tim out with the victim, just as the sun was setting.

Dave Cheesmond & the Wildboys

It wasn't only locals like Blanchard, Stark, and Wallace who were beginning to turn up the heat on Yamnuska in the early Eighties. Dave Cheesmond had come to Canada from South Africa and had met Urs Kallen at a party somewhere out near Chestermere Lake in 1982. They climbed Mount Edith Cavell together, and Urs showed Cheesmond some of his photographic library of alpine prospects, such as the east face of Assiniboine. Climbing the variation to *Bottleneck Direct* with Urs on August 2, 1982 was perhaps the first time Cheesmond climbed on Yam.

Urs suggests that Dave was a much hotter climber before he immigrated to Canada, but that there had been some kind of accident; he'd broken his hip and couldn't stem any more. Chris Perry is more generous. He maintains that, "Dave Cheesmond was a lot better than everybody else. Those guys—the Wildboys—they weren't scared of putting in the odd one or two bolts, whereas most of us were locked into that 'no bolts' thing. The reason we were stuck into that was because we thought 'We're not at the top of climbing and therefore we don't feel justified in making that break with tradition.' Cheese was at the top of climbing, and if he needed one he didn't need any justification from anybody else!"

For a man who was to become a partner in a climbing equipment retail enterprise—Wildboys Sports in Calgary—his gear was always old-fashioned and tattered to the point of failure. However, Dave's force of personality was what held any team he was a part of together. He was invariably positive, full of energy and competitive. He had a constant and heavy alpine agenda, but he was eager to make his mark on pure rock climbs as well. Early on he asked Chris Perry, "What's the hardest route?" When he was given an answer, he immediately went and repeated John Lauchlan and Bruce Keller's *The Maker* in the CMC Valley behind Yamnuska. There was suddenly a

Dave Cheesmond. Photo Kevin Doyle.

"The most superb climber to ever be in these parts."
(Urs Kallen, talking about Dave Cheesmond)

sense of comparison, a rivalry of reputation, between Cheesmond and Lauchlan [the latter was killed attempting to solo *Polar Circus* in February of 1982, shortly after Cheesmond arrived]. A free ascent of Brian Greenwood's imposing *Balrog*, likely the first, followed almost immediately for Dave. This ugly climb was to be an indicator of many others to come. For Cheesmond the moves needed to be bold; the rock was bad and the line was uncertain and run-out above dubious protection.

It is difficult to say today if it was Stark and Wallace's freeing of *CMC Wall* in 1984 that renewed popular interest in Yamnuska. Whatever the incentive, and whether that critical climb might truly have been the motivating factor, Cheesmond and his partners were drawn back to the crag like moths to a light in the season immediately following Stark and Wallace's feat. The summers of 1985 and 1986 were to become unquestionably the greatest and wildest times the "climbed-out" piece of rock would ever see.

"Gross was impressive, but reckless. Cheesmond pushed both people and standards. I remember Cheesmond and Doyle climbing up to us on the 3rd pitch of Necromancer. He joined us at the stance and brought Doyle up using an unanchored body belay. We went down. They waited out a snowstorm there and did the second free ascent."
(Andy Genereux)

To introduce the rest of the cast of key players, it might be best to begin with another South African: Brian Gross was a soft-spoken hard man—a friend of Cheesmond's who also arrived on the Calgary scene around 1981. Some have called him "the designated hitter" of the Wildboys, maintaining it was Gross who took the sharp end of the climbing whenever the going got truly difficult or dangerous during those big years. To be sure, Gross never backed away from a challenge, though he occasionally erred in the other direction—pushing himself to the point where he suffered serious serial injuries in pursuit of a purer climbing experience.

Never was that climbing experience more distilled than in the climbs that were done over the summers of 1985 and 1986. During those two intense seasons, Gross was an integral part of the first ascents of *The Heat Is On*, *Brown Trousers*, *The Wild Boys*, *Astro Yam*, and *Above and Beyond*. Any one of those routes, taken today, could represent the absolute pinnacle of a lesser climber's life.

Choc Quinn was the anchor of the group. He is a big Irishman casually mythologized for his enormous appetite for potatoes and other simple food. Over the years many stories have been told with a shake of the head following episodes where he supposedly showed up for a weekend's climbing with a single packet of Ramen noodles, declaring, "I've got the soup, then," and looking expectantly at everyone else. He was, nevertheless, much sought after to backstop desperate efforts on the rocks. The other rock stars might have their moments of youthful brilliance, but Quinn was always there to catch them when they fell, or carry the day with his stubborn attitude whenever conditions took a turn for the worse.

Quinn had come to Canada following a climb on Denali in 1981 and stayed on in Vancouver to work as an engineer rather than return to Ireland. He was transferred to Calgary and became immediately immersed in the local scene, doing difficult rock climbs in the Bow Valley between alpine forays in the Rockies and abroad.

Choc Quinn.
Photo CMC collection.

Above right: Dave Cheesmond.
Photo Barry Blanchard.

"Brian Gross was 'The Man.' Sort of like Ian Heys—it doesn't matter where the route goes—he'll climb it anyhow."
(Urs Kallen)

Brian Gross.
Photo CMC collection.

The Heat Is On

In 1985, schedules, attitudes and ambitions combined to bring Quinn, Gross, and Cheesmond together for what is now recognized as the trilogy—three new climbs, exacting and dangerous, executed in quick succession in a single season. It was a performance that pointed the way to a whole new kind of climbing on Yamnuska.

The first of these landmark routes was called *The Heat Is On*, after a popular music theme of the day and because the trio's work on the line was begun in May of 1985 on a bitterly cold day.

Tim Auger climbed this "out-there" route with Joe Josephson in a rare repeat ascent a decade later. The rock bears strong similarities to *Kahl Wall*, Tim says, which he did with Vockeroth on the first ascent many years before, climbing through the same sequence of stuff. "You had to use your absolute maximum antennae to figure out just which way you were going to go. And the pro is so thin and you're just going on … The description of the route says 5.9 or 5.10a, and you have to use all the little tricks that you need of constantly looking sideways looking over your shoulder for what might be the way. Before you commit yourself, you have to be absolutely certain that this is it.

"They didn't have a road map at all, those guys. They would have done it without the advantage of knowing, when they plunged in, that this was actually going to work. So everybody who climbs *The Heat Is On* admires the route for that. Because it's right on the limit of what you can keep doing with enough ease that you can risk going on without pro. It's run-out; it's a real mind trip. I managed to lead most of it because I had the tricks—the tools.

"And then you're at the crux section of the climb; you can shout, but the rope goes around the corner and hangs down over an overhang to the belay somewhere in another world. And you're up there on your own. I remember this water-washed, compact-type limestone and the route description is, 'you will come to a bolt.' You're climbing and looking and climbing and looking and waiting and finally there it is. Everybody who has been there knows the one I'm talking about. You're in this kind of Cyclops-eye bowl-shaped steep feature and this single crappy Rawl bolt with a loose hanger spinning around on it. You look at it and go, 'Oh, fuck … is that all I get after all this?!' And the hard move is right after that —it's a borderline 5.10 move—it's thin stuff, a little bit frictiony, thin face holds. Your only pro is that bolt and you don't want to need it now you're so far out that you go, 'Well, there ain't no going back 'cause I'm not going to hang on that and lower out and there's a couple of holds here and the only ones that can be and they've got to go because they must have before so you go and you do it. It's quite a ways to where it all starts to come back and you get something decent in. You definitely feel good when you finish a pitch like that—it's the essence of climbing on Yamnuska—*The Heat Is On* is a great name because the adrenaline is definitely on!"

Following *Heat*, in June of 1985 Cheesmond, Gross, and Quinn completed *Brown Trousers* after several attempts, once again creating a difficult and bold route with uncertain run-outs and variable rock quality. Like the others, the climb has seen only a handful of ascents in the years since it was first put up, despite being adjacent to the incredibly popular *Red Shirt* route that its name plays on. The only aid on the climb—a tension traverse—was eliminated during a revisitation of the route by Brian Gross, returning to the scene of his earlier crime in the company of Jeff Marshall and Jeff Everett.

Lastly came *The Wild Boys*, completed finally in the heat of August near the end of that impressive summer. The climb finds some slight shelter from the sun in slender corners to the right of *Balrog*. The Wildboys was the three's pet name for themselves and their small group of friends and active

Calgary climbers, celebrated on the rock of Yamnuska. In keeping with their committed style, the 6th pitch of the route demanded run-out, difficult climbing high above a single belay bolt. The line has seen little traffic since.

That same summer of 1985, on a less successful occasion, Brian Gross had become confused about where the classic *Direttissima* began, and had scrambled to a piton on a pedestal below a blank feature known locally as Suicide Wall. Looking up, he thought he saw potential on the face above. But when he mentioned the idea for a new route on Suicide Wall back in the pub, he was laughed at. So "naturally, we were up there again first thing next season!"

Dave Cheesmond.
Photo Kevin Doyle.

Jeff Marshall and Astro Yam

"I was never one of the Cheesmond gang, really— one of the Wildboys."
(Jeff Marshall)

As a boy, growing up in Calgary, Jeff Marshall would boulder. A lot. He was taking this climbing thing seriously, working on ever-more-difficult moves at Okotoks Rock south of the city. Though strong, Jeff had avoided roped climbing for the first years after beginning to scramble with his outdoor class in junior high. But in his own words, Marshall "appreciated the recognition" that climbing gave him as a youngster and he gradually transferred his attentions to bigger objectives. In those pre-sport-climbing days, an up-and-comer's choices were limited to the alpine for rock climbing. And the most accessible among those options was Yamnuska. It was 1978 and Jeff was sixteen years old.

In 1981, at the relatively young age of 19, Marshall hooked up with Brian Wallace and managed the unheralded third ascent of *CMC Wall*. Gradually, his enthusiasm built, and on an almost weekly basis Jeff found himself returning to the cliff for early free attempts on *Necromancer* and several other routes. He was often in the company of Barry Blanchard.

Today, Jeff Marshall still has a book—a large-format, blue-ruled accountant's ledger—that he can walk down the hall in his house in Calgary and retrieve from a back room. In it he has recorded all of the dates, climbs, and partners that have made up his life for the last twenty years. This book claims he only REALLY began climbing on Yamnuska in '86 with the first ascent of the incredible *Astro Yam*. It was a route that proved to be a breakthrough, a watershed in the perception of what comprised a line on Yamnuska and the style in which it should be climbed.

Many different people were involved with the big project over the weeks during the spring of 1986 while the climb was being considered and explored. Any number had speculated about the proposed line— or lack thereof—on what became known colloquially as Suicide Wall. Wallace and

Jeff Marshall. Photo Steve DeMaio.

Opposite: Jeff Marshall leading pitch 2 of *Astro Yam*. Photo Steve DeMaio.

Geoff Powter had been on the route. Chees-mond had taken a look as well. Altogether, there might have been perhaps five or six efforts prior to the day Gross headed up to the crag with Marshall. Steve DeMaio, newly arrived in town and looking for any action he could find, was a late addition to the party, making it a threesome.

The methods Gross and Marshall wanted to employ marked a clear departure from the way new rock climbs had been put up previously on Yamnuska, and in the Canadian Rockies generally. Natural breaks—the cracks, corners and chimneys that had been sought out and linked together to make steep climbs—were for the first time abandoned in favour of the open, unknown faces on the smooth, scary expanses of stone in between.

Marshall says that the team that day had been inspired by reports of the techniques employed by people like John Bachar in California. Bachar was a prominent, controversial talent who had begun establishing protection on featureless new free climbs around Joshua Tree and Tuolumne Mead-ows by hanging from a daisy-chain attached to sky hooks, thus allowing him free hands to drill holes for permanent anchors. These hooks were an esoteric artificial-aid device employed to find purchase behind tiny flakes or on small edges. Bachar, and thence Marshall, Gross, DeMaio, and eventually many others would climb while carrying a bit, holder, and hammer, and when the time came for placing protection, if there were no cracks to afford a piton or wired nut or camming device, would attempt to set a hook on some minute irregularity. They could then hang to drill a hole in the rock, and place a bolt by hand. Intrigued by the method's potential, Marshall and Gross wondered what it would allow them to piece together.

Ultimately, the key to what would come to be called *Astro Yam* (opening the way to the upper reaches of the wall) proved to be the inspired 5th pitch (as described in the topo contained in the current *Bow Valley Rock*, the first ascent party counted it the 4th). Marshall moved up from the belay on compact rock, drilled a bolt, moved up a bit more, drilled again, and then cast off on what rapidly became a nightmare of obscure holds that seemingly went on forever. He would be unable to stop until almost the full length of the rope had been run out.

Glenn Reisenhofer, one of Jeff's regular partners in later years, reckons the feat one of the great moments in Yam history: "I think it was pretty ballsy when Marshall led the crux pitch on *Astro Yam*. Jeff had no concept of its difficulty ahead of time and he faced it straight on, one on one. Was he out of his mind? Maybe. I think that this lead was bold, and slightly deranged."

Today, Marshall reflects on that specific stretch of desperate, intricate, down-sloping climbing, and flatly states, "I was totally frightened almost the whole time! I had no idea of what to think about it all when I was finished. Gross graded it after seconding."

And with that amazing display of tenacity the way was open. The three were soon howling from the top of the new route.

"I think it was pretty ballsy when Marshall led the crux pitch on Astro Yam. Jeff had no concept of its difficulty ahead of time and he faced it straight on, one on one. Was he out of his mind? Maybe. I think that this lead was bold, and slightly deranged."
(Glenn Reisenhofer)

The Bolting Ethic Evolves

The prevailing sentiment in Canadian climbing into the Eighties contained a stubborn commitment to the minimization of fixed or permanent hardware. The idea of bolts placed in the rock on climbs was generally held to be repellent. Although developments in Europe and the United States had demonstrated that great advances in difficulty could be surmounted with the use of more advanced methods, and although there was some quiet endorsement of these aids for artificial climbing on extremely steep or 'impossible' ground, many in Canada considered it "cheating" or "bad style" to place expansion bolts, drilled directly into the rock, for the purpose of making a free climb safer or more convenient.

Chris Perry believes the anti-bolt ethic was imported from England. "It's important in England, but though the ethic is not really applicable here, it was so ingrained that it was always applied."

Like anything that makes things easier, cheaper, and safer, the use of bolts gradually spread, and specific pieces became accepted. "*Kahl Wall* has bolts, though it's not really the same style as everyone else was climbing. There's a bolt on *Chockstone Corner* at the crux pitch, bolts on *Balrog*, where there were originally three that were drilled for aid.

"The really groundbreaking route as far as bolts were concerned was *The Maker*. They thought, '*The Maker*—it's like Glacier Point Apron in Yosemite, only it's limestone and it's forty degrees steeper, but it's the same idea—it's blank, you can't do it unless you put bolts in. And then of course they were good climbers, at the top of climbing. Because when you are at the top of climbing you can justify a decision like that—'Nobody else is going to do it, so why don't I do it with a bolt?' It doesn't use many and they were put in on lead, and it's certainly not a sport route by any stretch of the imagination."

Chris Perry. Photo Gillean Daffern.

Perry explains that *Astro Yam*, when it came in 1986, was the same as *The Maker* in this respect: "It's the absolute minimum to prevent a death fall. You would certainly take a big whipper." But it was "a huge leap in difficulty. Instead of 5.9, it's now 11b. So basically you've got people who are really bold and really good, but they're not totally stupid—they've got to put one or two bolts in.

"That was the real ground-breaking route, though. Before that, there was *Brown Trousers*, and *Wild Boys* at 10c, 10d. Before that *Kahl Wall*, *High Voltage*, or *Balrog* free at 10a.

"It [*Astro Yam*] was a huge jump in standards and it wouldn't have been possible without some bolts. So—a really definitive route. That change was not really transferred to Yamnuska until *Astro Yam*."

"It was holding things up so much, not to put bolts in." (Chris Perry)

101

The Dynamic Duo

The summer of 1986 was far from over, however. It was destined to be a season submerged under wave after wave of big climbs. And a major injection of the energy that would drive it came from another newcomer to the scene.

Steve DeMaio was 14 in 1978 when he tried his hand at rock climbing. Shortly thereafter, in 1981, he did his first new route on an 25-metre Ontario cliff. There Steve had conscientiously adopted a specific ground-up style despite the ease with which he could have gone round to the top of the climb. Partly as a result of this decision he took a ten-metre fall. Still, the seminal experience showed him that exploring virgin rock was his preferred approach to the climbing game.

When he eventually saw the Rockies a few years later, the front ranges in general and Yamnuska in particular looked like heaven to Steve. It was 1985 and he was 21 when he first ventured onto the rock of Yamnuska during an autumn visit from his home in Burlington, Ontario. Struggling with bad information and an old guidebook, he and his partner were unable to locate the classic *Forbidden Corner*, and made an ascent of *Pangolin* instead. Despite their difficulties, gazing out from the belays on the cliff, and walking along the base after their climb was a big experience for climbers brought up on the Niagara Escarpment. Steve says that he was "freaking out at the limestone walls" and the sheer extent of rock waiting to be climbed.

Yam became the dream for Steve, and he decided to move west and treat it like the rock of Ontario, where he had established many, many new routes. A climbing friend in whom he confided this ambition told him "Good luck …"

Arriving in Calgary on Monday, May 3, 1986, Steve immediately went to the Mountain Equipment Co-op store to ask about routes on Yamnuska and to get directions to any local bouldering. It was well-met that day, when a clean-cut DeMaio, fresh from the flats of the mid-continent, was sent over to talk to a compact guy with wire-rimmed glasses and a ponytail, standing behind the equipment counter.

Marshall responds that at that first meeting he initially picked the Easterner for another "climbing shop loser." All the while DeMaio was thinking, "Christ, another guy with a head so big he needs a bandana!"

Self portrait by Steve DeMaio.

After introductions, Marshall carefully advised the newcomer that "You'll have to shave a few grades off your expectations—this is climbing on limestone, you know." [Steve had been climbing on nothing but limestone in Ontario.] Despite their mutual reservations, the two met again when Marshall got off work to boulder at Okotoks Rock. They agreed to "stay in touch."

Over the next few weekdays, DeMaio finally located and rope-soloed *Forbidden Corner*, in the snow. Then came the May long-weekend, and DeMaio's new friends hooked him up with the energetic Bill Betts. The two climbed *Smeagol*, *Pangolin*, and *Missionary's Crack*, all in one day. On the next day, still restless and with no other prospects, DeMaio tagged along with Brian Gross and Marshall on what would be the landmark first ascent of *Astro Yam*. Steve says, "My fingers were sore, and they wouldn't hold the little edges."

Things were only beginning to pick up speed, however. Betts said he had the line for the following weekend. A short six days later the two returned to a spot on the right side of *The Bowl* and in what has been said to be possibly the greatest day of climbing ever seen on the cliff, did the first ascent of *East End Boys* in 12 hours.

Steve, telling the story: "Both of us were on fire—that day was a religious experience! I put 7 wires in under the big roof. I'd just taken this 80-foot screamer where I'd actually fallen PAST Bill's belay. Bill comes up, looks at the roof, looks at the stance ... I ask him if he's done much aid. Bill says, 'Don't ask me that question NOW!'" They hammered in a bolt.

> *"This was a tough and memorable lead by Bill close to the end of a hard day."*
> *(Steve DeMaio describing the 6th pitch on East End Boys.)*

Steve DeMaio and Jeff Marshall. Photo Steve DeMaio.

> *"We were full of confidence."*
> *(Jeff Marshall)*

"That was the Saturday—on Sunday I was back up there for the second free ascent of *CMC Wall*."

When Betts and DeMaio returned to town and Bill told Urs Kallen what they had done, the phlegmatic Swiss suggested, "You two should never climb together again." He was almost prophetic.

The two men planned to go out on the next Thursday, and Steve had booked the day off work already when Betts called to cancel. Somewhat frustrated, DeMaio hiked up to Yamnuska by himself. He went directly to a crack line he'd spotted from the long belays on *Astro Yam* a week earlier. Beginning at 5 am and finishing as the last rays of the sun shone over the summit of Yamnuska, he carried the almost completely independent line of *Highlander* totally alone, from the scree to the rim of the cliff. He climbed, rappelled, and jumared every pitch, taking out the gear he had placed. It was an amazing feat of concentration, confidence and skill.

The first ascent of *East End Boys*. Bill Betts leaving the belay to begin pitch 6, 5.10 A2. Photo Steve DeMaio

Steve claims he never felt more empowered on a mountain than on that day, and named the route after the popular B movie of the period about the self-discovery and trials of an immortal warrior. Confiding in Joe Josephson years later, he slyly insisted that in order to obtain the full experience on the route a leader must throw his head back when at the lip of the penultimate roof and howl, "There can be only one!"

The following weekend Brian Gross told Steve, "I've got another project, left of *Balrog.*"

"On the Saturday, I'm at the first stance, with no gear in because it's supposed to be casual and Gross is out 60 feet. And he pulls a big block off! It nails my leg! The pain is incredible. We go down, go to town, and have me checked over.

"We go back the next day, Sunday. I break the driver after one bolt. Brian pops a hook, tags the ledge on his way by—breaking his ankle—and factor-twos onto the belay! Brian is totally calm through this kind of thing.

One time I heard him say, 'I refuse to run it out more than 25 feet between pieces—I'm getting too old.' Anyway, I shuttled him down the trail to the parking lot, alternating carrying him and going back for the packs. After visiting the hospital the evening before for my leg, we're in Foothills again. Brian says, 'Maybe we should call this route "Wildboys Go To Hospital."'"

"Jeff and I had two more tries. Then Gross took off his cast in the bathtub and we went up there in August. He's leading the 6th pitch and he falls again! But THIS time the rope is caught by some blocks on a ledge, and he's saved from breaking anything else! In the end we just called the route *Above and Beyond.*"

Taken in its entirety, *Above and Beyond* was a harder climb than *Astro Yam*—more technical and more dangerous—but the tape had been cut, and the wrapper was off, and despite being only a few months younger, the route did not extend the controversy its precursor had begun.

Brian Gross and Steve DeMaio jumar on *Above and Beyond*. Photo Jeff Marshall.

The victorious team after *Above and Beyond*. Left to right: Steve DeMaio, Brian Gross, Jeff Marshall. Photo Steve DeMaio collection.

Many, many more routes would come from the pairing of Steve DeMaio and Jeff Marshall, who by this time had known each other for only three months. Jeff says of *Above and Beyond*, and also of their other outings, "Steve would specialize, it seemed, and got most of the crack and corner pitches—I got the stupid face shit. The names on most of the routes, those ones that year [in 1986] anyway, were mine, though. I guess I was jabbing against the sport climbers."

In 1987 DeMaio was back to contribute *Trap Line*, a long route sweeping the crag to the right of *Kahl Wall*. He and his partner, Ward Robinson, had earlier been hoping to climb the monstrous north face of North Twin near the Columbia Icefield, but "we didn't get very far." Dave Cheesmond was lost on the Hummingbird Ridge of Mount Logan that same spring.

Back again with Jeff Marshall in 1988, the two got up on Yamnuska very early in the season and finished *Excalibur* in April before most climbers in the area had even returned to the rock after the winter. "It was COLD!" DeMaio says. "There was snow around. Our hands were numb. Jeff's 45 feet off the station with no protection. I'm freaking, and dropping extra coils and winding them around blocks on the ledge I'm on. Then he looks down at me and he says, 'Hey, James? Do you have the hooks?'

"Why was it always like this?! But, that was Jeff. He did an amazing job—it was incredible work putting in that bolt."

Marshall is more concise in his description of the experience. He says simply that *Excalibur* came after the two had gone to climb Mount Fable, north of Exshaw. They had turned around and returned to Yamnuska because of difficult conditions. "So we one-timed that in the snow on April 1."

Competition and Criticism

Not everybody involved with the climbing scene at the time found such displays of confidence attractive. Shepard Steiner, when the conversation can be dragged away from everything else in the world and back onto the subject of himself, allows that he began climbing on Yam in 1977 or '78, in the company of an Alpine Club of Canada leadership training group. He was forced to travel long distances to the mountains because he was living in Edmonton at the time.

Shep's alpine education took another tentative step the following year when he led (leading for the first time) his three cousins, all four tied together on a short 40-metre rope, on a 12-hour epic ascent—"hammering like, seven pitons into every pitch"—of *Grillmair Chimneys*. He laughs.

Steiner was a considerably better climber when he and fellow Edmontonian Roger Keglowich climbed *Freak Out* in 1984 or '85. They believed theirs to be the long-awaited second ascent of the dangerous Davidson/Horne route. Despite pioneering a number of more difficult and technically demanding routes on Yamnuska in the years since, Steiner asserts that his and Roger's confrontation of this desperate psychological test is still one of the climbs of which he is most proud. At the time it was a mark of commitment to the cliff.

A short while later, Shep moved to Banff and was hanging out with an aggressive crowd of young moderns who were setting standards both in the alpine and on the newly evolving sport-climbing scene in the canyons of the Bow Valley. It was a high-spirited era with the scent of competition in the air. In reaction to what the Banff-based crowd felt was excessive breast-beating by the original ascent party, he teamed with Keith Haberl in the summer of '88 to rapidly re-climb the "supposedly" standard-breaking *Astro Yam*.

Once on the rock and working from information provided by their friend Colin Zacharias, they made quick progress to the

"Today, he admits the crux is likely at least 11b. But at the time, flushed with their success, the two down-rated the moves to a mere 10d and for a while referred to the route publicly as 'Astro Sham.'

"Understandably, such counterclaims did not sit well with the proud Calgary crowd."

Shep Steiner. Photo Shep Steiner collection.

crux run-out on the 5th pitch where, Steiner calmly says, "I fell where you didn't want to fall. I went too high and traversed left and something broke." Happily, he was caught by a tri-cam inserted in a shallow hole a few metres above the critical bolts that began the run-out face. It was a placement that the original trio hadn't made, and it saved Steiner from a much, much longer drop.

Because "me and Keith were adamant that we were going to lead ALL the pitches properly, and then downgrade the climbing," Steiner lowered to a previous hands-down rest on a little pillar partway up the pitch. He untied, then pulled the rope down through the protection he had clipped on his first attempt, tied in to the end of the rope again, and climbed the pitch cleanly. Today, he admits the crux is likely at least 11b. But at the time, flushed with their success, the two down-rated the moves to a mere 10d and for a while referred to the route publicly as "Astro Sham."

Understandably, such counterclaims did not sit well with the proud Calgary crowd. Partly because of an unrelated episode involving the chipping of an artificial training climb in nearby Grotto Canyon, and fuelled by other confrontations and comments, an enmity blossomed that partitioned the local community and took years to dissipate. Most of the details have been forgotten, or anyway disputed, but they still echo through the opinions of some. Steiner, for example, maintains that "*Yellow Edge* is the grizzliest of Yam classics," whereas most Calgary climbers who were active during the Eighties feel that the first free ascent of that route in January of 1986 was "stolen" by Steiner's friend Colin Zacharias and imported West Coast talent Peter Croft, and that *Astro Yam* was the real, true catalyst for further explorations on the cliff.

A Visit from the Sunny Side of the Alps

No matter how much a hero one might feel, or how big a frog in the smaller home pond, there are always those other people from those other places who can help you keep your perspective. In June of 1988, Bojan Pokar and Nejc Skof, two visiting alpinists from Slovenia, arrived, climbed a bold new route on Yamnuska, then left the area just as quickly. The scant information available says they accomplished their climb almost casually, hiking up to the cliff, picking a line and dispatching the route in a reported five hours. They were clearly bringing the big-mountain mentality to the crag—one that placed the greatest value on speed, efficiency, and simply getting to the top. Their route quite obviously sought out the line of greatest weakness and the easiest and quickest passage from the place where they began at the bottom of the crag to the rim. There was much scrambling and many easier passages along the arcing series of corners they followed, but the way chosen looks to be steeper than nearby routes, and the final three pitches are now known to be of a better quality—albeit less direct—than the finish to the adjacent *Dazed and Confused*.

It was an impressive accomplishment, achieved in an almost offhanded fashion, and could have served as a bit of a lesson for the locals. Never had a route of that high a standard been climbed for the first time, in less time, in the history of the cliff. Few Calgary climbers, however, even knew of their rapid passage. The pair left only a simplified sketch of their route in the logbook at the Alpine Club of Canada's clubhouse and a terse description of their climb with Chic Scott.

Opposite: Shep Steiner on *Verstiegenheit*.
Photo Todd Guyn.

The Bumblebee

Throughout the mid-Eighties, a number of people had been working off and on to exploit the potential left of *CMC Wall*. In '88, in the same season that he and Steve DeMaio climbed *Excalibur*, Jeff Marshall went up to the cliff with Andy Genereux (who had begun the project when he got lost beginning *CMC Wall* years before) and subsequently established the still exceptional *General Pain*.

When the story of Yamnuska has been told, Andy Genereux's name has been neglected repeatedly. This shortfall might be simply because the role he plays in the mountain's history is yet to be concluded. Andy has been climbing hard on Yam for almost three decades, putting up standard-setting routes while he watches others come and learn and climb and retire again. Genereux was not in the least a tag-along or relegated to any sort of support position with the *General Pain* project. Indeed, the climb had been his idea from the very beginning.

Andy's first experience on Yamnuska was as a student from Bishop Carroll High School in Calgary. It was also his first rock climb ever: *Unnamed*, led by Ben Gadd in 1974. Genereux's first lead on Yamnuska was an attempt on the intimidating *Missionary's Crack*, which at the time of his rookie attempt in 1975 still enjoyed a fearsome reputation. He and his partner concluded their day by abandoning most of their rack to facilitate a retreat from higher on the route. "I think Chic Scott got it all in the end." [Urs Kallen claims it wasn't Chic, but "somebody else."]

Partnering with Joe Frey, Andy joined the CMC in 1976. He had reached a stage where he was soloing laps on many of the easy routes on Yamnuska and was looking for a more intense and demanding experience. Then for a while Andy lost his enthusiasm. He abruptly quit climbing following a scary alpine experience on Mount Edith Cavell. The stress had been compounded by coming across an awful, multiple-fatality car wreck on the way to the climb.

A young Andy Genereux on *Red Shirt*.
Photo Joe Frey.

Drilling on *General Pain*. Photo Andy Genereux collection.

The overhang on *General Pain*. Photo Andy Genereux.

It was Bill Rennie, a friend of Andy's from university wrestling, who persuaded him to begin climbing again. The two got together for a simple ascent of Bear's Hump above Waterton townsite. Andy was quickly hooked again and spent much of the Eighties climbing with Rennie. Early during this period, back on Yam, the two did what was possibly the first or second free ascent of *Balrog* (also variously attributed to Cheesmond, Friesen, et al).

Picking up the timeline, Andy says, "*Spring Fever* was the first new route I did on Yam. I'd put in the first pitch rope solo in January of that year—it was a dry winter—then did the rest with Jones in March." Genereux had met Jon Jones through Bill Rennie and Jones' girlfriend at the time, Mary Lynn Parr, a woman who worked with Rennie. Thus, with *Spring Fever* in 1987, was begun a partnership that would go on to produce many landmark routes throughout the front ranges of the Rockies, and see the development of several exceptional sport-climbing venues.

But before all that would come *General Pain*. Prior to 1988, Genereux says he talked incessantly with the likes of Brian Wallace and others about doing hard free climbs and difficult single pitches. He believes he accomplished an early free ascent of *CMC Wall*, possibly the fourth or the fifth, with Rob Lanthier as a result of these conversations. "We got lost and did the first two pitches of what would become *General Pain*. Then I came back with Jeffrey [Marshall] and spent maybe two years before it was finished. I think it might still be the hardest route on Yam, just because of its mixed free and aid."

During his work on the line, Genereux came close to killing himself one day by miscalculating the friction after switching to a single-strand rappel while attempting to reach the ground on the final leg of a descent. He lost control of the rope with a heavy load of gear on his back and slid free for 20 metres while frantically trying to arrest his fall. He was caught when the knot he had tied in the end of the cord jammed in his rappel setup. Luckily, he'd failed in his original intention and the strand hadn't reached all the way to the bottom—he was stopped a shockingly short two metres off the deck!

The pair's final push took them two days. A bivouac was part of the plan, but was an experience that Genereux feels there is no need to repeat. "We didn't have enough water, and were undersupplied with bolts. Now I bail off things like that at a predetermined point."

Today, though the top of the climb sees traffic as the second half of *Master Mind*, the first section is usually avoided because of a large loose block on the 3rd pitch. Detached on three sides, this geologic time bomb apparently threatens the belay and would cause unimaginable havoc if it were to come loose with a party committed to the pitch.

General Pain passed immediately into obscurity, unfortunately—the route was completed only a few months too late to be included in Chris Perry's inspirational *Bow Valley Rock*, co-authored with John Martin and Sean Dougherty, which was published by Rocky Mountain Books earlier in 1988. This guidebook was the first to treat Yamnuska compendiously since the Kallen pamphlet of 1977, and was the first ever to place the information in the context of rock climbing in the Bow Valley as a whole. The book was immediately and tremendously influential, encouraging many repeats of long-overlooked routes throughout the area and goading the next generation of Yamnuska climbers into action. So much new activity was generated that *Bow Valley Update*, from Perry, Martin and Jon Jones, was needed only three years later in 1991. *General Pain* was included at that time, lost among hundreds of other new routes representing the burgeoning sport-climbing boom.

Banging the Drum Slowly

By 1989 the spirit of the whole mad venture was beginning to change for Marshall and DeMaio. While another big new line was established with the ascent of *Jimmy and the Kid*, Steve felt that the edge had dulled with the death of Brian Wallace. Their friend had been killed in their company during an attempt on the north face of Mount Lougheed, and *'the Kid* stood more as a memorial and as a stubborn return to their old arena for Jeff and him. This time there was no howling from the top of the cliff when they finished. "It was different for me. I also had tendonitis that year."

Marshall doesn't have much to say about this route except that it was "hard, scary, and run-out. I don't know—11d A3? Steve jumared the face pitch. There's no bloody way I could ever do that again!" Sections of loose rock complicate the serious nature of the climbing. For probably very good reasons the route stands unrepeated today.

Almost as an afterthought, in 1989 DeMaio also climbed *The Quickening* with John Kaandorp, a visiting friend from Ontario. The opening of the route went relatively uneventfully, perhaps profiting from Steve's previous experience on the adjacent rock of *Yellow Edge*. Today, he believes the line of *The Quickening* to be worthwhile primarily as a variation on that Kallen/Davidson route, though the climb currently stands in a state of some disrepair. Typically, as was his habit in those days, Steve took most of his hangers off after he'd placed and used the bolts.

In 1990 Steve came back for *Jimmy and the Cruisers*. First-time climbers on *Red Shirt* route had long been making the mistake of missing the leftward traverse that constitutes the 4th pitch on that climb, and continuing too high into the increasingly difficult corner above. This feature of the face was typically festooned with garlands of slings left at different highpoints, where frustrated leaders had finally looked over their shoulders, seen where they were SUPPOSED to be, and lowered off. Steve's re-

> *"I had told Jeff that you never drop a hook until you know it's bomber, or else the 'air' is clean." (Steve DeMaio)*

turn for *'Cruisers* made a virtue out of the popular error and carried the natural line up and right into steep clean faces and a committing rightward traverse.

Although there is brilliant climbing in the upper portion of *Jimmy and the Cruisers*, it was not easy to discover the way. Joe Josephson worked with Steve on the lower pitches, connecting corners from the left of *Red Shirt*, then DeMaio returned with Jeff Nazarchuk to link the upper section.

Steve says that in those days for that sort of a route, he would have been carrying perhaps only eight bolts in total, believing that number should be sufficient to see the team through to the top of the cliff. So it came to pass that after a long afternoon of difficult progress, at the stance after pitch 5, the duo was hanging there with three bolts remaining. It was 5 pm and behind them lay much 5.10 climbing. Above was 15 metres of blank face and, because of the traversing nature of the line and overhangs below, it was not at all clear that the two could escape via rappel if they were not up to the task ahead. Luckily, the wall that guarded the top of *'Cruisers* gave up beautiful incut holds that came to hand just when they were needed and the tension gradually evaporated. The story could have ended very differently.

Over the years this climb has received much praise from successive ascent parties. And yes, DeMaio did take the hangers from his bolts here, too. Several of those early repeat attempts became epic retreats before success was realized. But if you go to tackle the route today, all the hangers are in situ on the climb, and it stands as one of the more popular of the modern classics.

As this was happening, DeMaio, ever the king of projects, had been working on yet another line that began on *Astro Yam* and split right to forge straight up through steep new ground. Begun in 1987, the project that earned the cynically applied name *Quantum Leap* had seen Steve partnered with many of Yamnuska's best players over any number of forays. Early on he had begun exploration with Dave Fisher. Later he pushed ahead pitch by pitch in various combinations with Frank Campbell, Choc Quinn, Jeff Marshall and others. On one attempt the team was repulsed when DeMaio, sleepless after a hard evening of socializing, lost his bolt driver and had to manufacture an extremely tentative anchor from which to lower off. Dispirited, he was ready to head for the parking lot when Choc, his partner for the day, declared, "No way have I hiked up here to climb one pitch! Cheesmond would roll over in his grave!" Quinn insisted they 'run' up *Direttissima* before he would allow the team to turn for home.

Finally, the summer of 1990 saw completion of the climb, once again with Steve tied in with Jeff Marshall. The two friends slept in hammocks, drilled on lead, and extended a mixed free and aid line through the excitingly blank terrain between *Astro Yam* and *Above and Beyond*. The new route was given its name after Marshall snatched and missed while six unprotected metres up the 4th pitch, and fell with almost full factor-two force onto DeMaio's belay.

"I was incoherent. Thank God we had a policy of bolting all our stations when the going got blank!

"With Jeff, there was going to be no fooling around. It was like when he decided that we'll take bivi gear—we're gonna be ready. So then it snows while we're bivied up on the route. And we rap AGAIN.

"There was always something. On the way down I had to take a huge swing, coming off, carrying two packs, running across the face, to reach one of the stances."

Eventually, one last time that summer, the pair returned and bulled their way up the pitches, repeating the line and pressing through new ground toward the rim. But still, 15 metres from the top and in the dark once again, the team was struggling to finish. DeMaio took over the lead...

"We're rushing now, off I go, 30 feet up it's blank, it gets hard ... I've got to drill, but the edges are not good. I get one hook down, then eventually another off to the side around a bad nubbin. But the rock in front of me is hollow! I can't get a good angle to drill. It's horrible—it was a shift for me—from the old days. I used to love this stuff. Now I'm not so light-hearted about it any more. Bad drilling, the mosquitoes are bothering me, and I'm thinking, 'Fuck! This is a SERIOUS sport!'

"The next day I'm at work and I'm thinking, 'If that's what it takes.'

"Basically, I retired for seven years after that."

At present, the Marshall/DeMaio creation of *Quantum Leap* still awaits its second ascent, and remains one of the few routes on the cliff demanding aid techniques.

Marshall says of those heady days of the Eighties: "Coming up and coming out, you had the choice of the Alpine Club of Canada or the Calgary Mountain Club. I liked the CMC—life was pretty full-on. I had this impression that there were all these people ahead of me on the crag—the drive and foundation was that we had to meet the challenges of the previous generation. I was maybe content to live up to that—Steve was the one with the attitude, who was always pressing for new routes.

"In the end, Yam was this thing, and this place, that nurtured me, and this was the way, doing new routes, that I could give back to it."

Opposite: Jeff Marshall and Steve DeMaio on the first ascent of *Quantum Leap*. Photo Glenn Reisenhofer.

The Nineties

Running Laps

Jeff Marshall with his best friend Bennie.
Photo Chic Scott

"I had this vision you could do 10 routes on Yam in a day. " (Jeff Marshall)

As the energy for new routes wound down, Marshall began to express his interest in the area through enchainments and solos. During one of his better efforts of the period (Jeff is reading again from his ledger) on June 21, 1989, he and Glenn Reisenhofer climbed *Grillmair Chimneys*, *Kahl Wall*, *Forbidden Corner*, *Red Shirt* and *The Bowl*. "We were starting on *Pangolin*, with lots of day left, when Glenn said he couldn't take it any more."

Reisenhofer's take on the effort is slightly more colourful: "Ah yes, Jeff Marshall ... It was 100% totally his idea. I was the sucker who tried it with him. We tried on one of those long summer days. We soloed *Grillmair*, I led all of *Kahl Wall*—lots of simul-climbing. Jeff led all of *Forbidden Corner*—lots of simul-climbing. We soloed *Red Shirt*, and Jeff led *The Bowl. The Bow*l really beat us—WAY too physical. I started up *Pangolin* and admitted to Jeff that I no longer felt safe enough to lead and he replied that he too was 'wasted and wanted a tight rope like a girl.' Jeff discovered later that if you do NOT run down the back side and take your time you don't feel as wasted."

In '91 (still turning pages) Marshall linked *The Bowl* and *Smeagol*. Shortly thereafter he put together *Kahl Wall*, *The Bowl*, and *Pangolin*, again all before returning for work at 2 pm. "I had this vision you could do 10 routes on Yam in a day. Take that as a challenge, maybe, for the youth of today."

Consulting the ledger one more time, it is revealed that, on June 22, 1992, he climbed *Necromancer*, *Chockstone Corner*, and *Missionary's Crack*—925 metres of technical climbing—again all before 2 pm. That's not including the elevation gain in the hike up from the parking lot, or the scramble down the back of the crag after topping out on the routes!

The 1992 Head Injury on Red Shirt

Climbers on Yamnuska find themselves in trouble quite regularly. Though the mountain enjoys easy access, it is a dangerous place, where a party must deal with questionable rock, extremes of temperature, and tricky route-finding. Seldom does a year go by without some incident that causes injury, though few of these occasions have been so serious as to result in fatalities. Often, if the party is capable, they can be self-rescuing and attempt to get off the cliff and down the hill under their own power. Once in a while, however, a situation develops that is serious enough to warrant a full response from regional Park and Forestry staff. The 1992 evacuation from *Red Shirt* was a case in point.

This was a "manpower assist" for Tim Auger—helping out as a Parks Canada employee in support of Kananaskis Country staff, who were the primary responders in the incident. Tim was flown to the top of Yam as the light was fading. The victim had fallen on the final pitch of *Red Shirt* and hit his head quite badly. Though communicating, he wasn't making a lot of sense. After raising him to the top, the rescuers got the man onto a stretcher just as it was getting dark. Because there would be no flying until it was light again, and because they were concerned about his head injury, they decided to attempt evacuation to the highway as quickly as possible.

It was a long night carrying the stretcher down the mountain. The way across the back of Yam was steep, with patches of snow, and there were slippery sections. The rescuers used six to eight people to carry the stretcher, and needed to lower it straight down some of the snow patches, then carry it across sideways, then set up and lower it again. It was after midnight when they reached the east end of the face where the rock meets the ridge. They were trying to be as gentle as possible.

A large group came up and met the rescue party at the corner. They attached a wheel to the stretcher and proceeded down the ridge to pick up the easily angled trail that makes a long switchback to the northeast.

Auger was talking to the patient as they went, attempting to keep him awake and responding. Tim believes that patients can be susceptible to a sort of mild form of hypnosis and he told the victim that "he was riding along in a gondola, in a boat in Venice, on the waves."

"I said to the guy, 'What do you do?' and he answered right away. He said, 'I'm a farmer.' It wasn't 'til afterward that I found out he was a third-year medical student at the University of Calgary."

The rescuers brought the stretcher into the parking area just as the sun was coming up, delivering the victim to the ambulance at the same time had they waited for the helicopter in the morning. "We now know how long it takes to haul a stretcher carefully down the back side of Yamnuska."

"For all its steepness and for all the travelling on Yamnuska, it's actually still a relatively safe place…The steeper the climbing in some ways, the safer, if you are using protection. I'm sure that there have been countless slips and falls on Yamnuska that have never been recorded because they were arrested by the belay the way they were supposed to." (Tim Auger)

Andy Genereux. Photo Chic Scott.

"I did climb CMC Wall in it's original condition, and on the retrofit I cleaned most of the rivets with my nut tool, and several fixed pins including those on belays I removed with only a tug and no hammering. Let's not forget the last pitch was equipped with 30-year-old shoelaces. Those are all solid reasons for a retrofit."
(Andy Genereux)

Baby's Got New Shoes: The CMC Wall Goes Free—Again

In the early Nineties, *CMC Wall* still had a serious reputation for awkward, dangerous climbing. Davidson and Kallen had taken several adventurous episodes to put up the line, mostly on artificial aid. That was in 1972. In the rare subsequent ascents, climbers were forced to make extensive use of the gear the two had left in place, much of which was intended to support only body weight. Some of these items had been improvised from economical materials that had then stood out in the weather—winter and summer—for nearly twenty years. There were placements that incorporated rusty metal strapping purpose-designed for banding crates, and/or rotting perlon that had originally served as shoelaces!

Compounding the route's reputation and further contributing to the seriousness of the endeavour, it was put about by would-be hard men that all these factors, taken in combination with the steepness of the face, would make any attempt to retreat from high on the route impossible.

Jon Jones and Andy Genereux had come into possession of two huge laid ropes in 1989, acquired as surplus from the British Army. The grand concept (Genereux claims it was his idea—"I talked Jones into doing it") was to pack these 100-metre monsters to the top of the cliff and use them to descend the original line of *CMC Wall*, with the intention of performing some much-needed route maintenance—improving fixed gear, removing hazards, and replacing stations. It was felt that in many spots on the route the leftover aid placements did not follow the best or most convenient line for free climbing.

Although not really a new route, this quixotic project served as an example of community consciousness, indicating a standard to which all future work on Yamnuska could aspire. The basic idea was, in Jon Jones words, to "sort out" the climbing, so it could be enjoyed athletically without having to worry about bad gear.

Rob Lanthier traversing on pitch 5 of CMC Wall. Photo Andy Genereux.

To this end, Genereux and Jones humped their 30 kg packs containing both ropes and a huge load of tools and hardware up from the parking lot and around the back side trail to the summit of the mountain. They anchored their lines at the rim and began three huge 100-metre rappels down the face, working as they went to replace old gear left from earlier ascents. As they descended, they clipped in to the new pieces to hold themselves close to the overhanging rock.

On the upper pitches Genereux replaced every third rivet of the first ascent aid ladders with a bolt, usually beginning by simply pulling the original hardware out of the rock with his nut tool. The anchors that had

Andy Genereux on *CMC Wall* in 1992. Photo Jon Jones

been installed so laboriously at the last Davidson bivi during the final push in 1972, he says, broke off in his hands.

Probably because of their twisted construction, the ex-WD ropes acted like giant coil springs, creating incredible snarls whenever they were unloaded. To hear either man tell the story, it was an almost unbearable pain in the ass to untangle and retrieve the ropes each time they had to set up the next in their succession of rappels.

As Jones and Genereux moved down the cliff, the route clung to its reputation for being difficult to retreat from. By the time they were approaching the talus at the bottom, the two had descended so much overhanging ground that Andy says he swung away from the rock like a pendulum, "straight out for 150 feet!" when he released himself from the station at the top of the 1st pitch onto the ropes anchored to the top of pitch 2.

But the work needed very much to be done. With the retrofit came not only new safety, but also demystification. The detailed information that Jones brought down from the climb and subsequently published widely through a new edition of the Bow Valley guidebook made *CMC Wall* a born-again classic. The climbing was good, and now the route was a known quantity, sporting modern and reliable anchors. It received more ascents in its first new season than it had in all the years of its previous history.

Genereux came back the following year, in 1993, to add a series of direct pitches to the climb. He worked on lead once again rather than resort to rappel to explore the "new" ground. With only one battery for drilling the intended three rope-lengths worth of anchors, conservation of power was essential. Despite the mechanical advantage employed, some heady intervals remain between the bolts. Thus, Andy feels that no teeth were pulled with the reworking, and that today *CMC Wall* retains its status of one of the must-do routes on the cliff.

Jeff Everett. Photo Glenn Reisenhofer.

Introducing the 'Sport' Sensibility

Genereux's and Jones' updating of the anchors on *CMC Wall* marked the first stirrings
of a revolution that modern attitudes toward
the employment of expansion bolts would
bring to Yamnuska. In 1993, the same year
that Andy began carrying a power drill to
protect alternative pitches on established
routes, Jeff Everett was taking hand-drilling
on new routes to its logical extreme further
along the cliff.

Everett had made his first forays onto
Yamnuska in 1979 or 1980, but didn't return
to the cliff for a decade following. As he
says, "I waited ten years before I did another
route there, because I didn't want to go near
that frightening place again. Equipped with
Al Derbyshire's climbing lessons [Derby-
shire has long been an outdoor skills in-
structor at Mount Royal College in Calgary],
a new rope, six hexes, ten 'biners, a figure-
eight, a pair of full-shank leather boots, and
a friend whose outdoor experiences were
limited to deer hunting, fishing, and four-

wheeling, I headed up to the base of the
Grillmair Chimneys. Twelve hours (!) later
and a whole lot lighter (I remember being
massively dehydrated) we were done, and
for my friend I mean REALLY done—he
never climbed with me again.

"And I've always wanted to thank Al for
suggesting, 'It's a good route, and only
[UIAA climbing grade] F5.' I quickly learned
what the 'F' stands for."

By 1993 Everett had explored more
climbs on Yam. He had teamed with Dave
Campbell (also from Calgary) and the two
were working to build a line they were call-
ing *Gormenghast*—four difficult pitches
leading directly into the right-trending fi-
nale of *Chockstone Corner*. Everett believed
this project could run straight as an arrow
and join perfectly to *Chockstone* just before
that climb's crux, giving an outstanding way
to ascend the wall. Before he was able to
tackle the whole line later that same spring,
however, he was obliged to return three or
four times to install the required bolts above
the ledges left of *Grillmair Chimneys*. Then,

Glenn Reisenhofer. Photo Colleen Purtill.

Dave Campbell. Photo Dave Dornian.

Opposite: Glenn Reisenhofer approaching the crux on *Gormenghast*. Photo Jeff Everett.

after all his effort, while attempting the first complete ascent, he found he had to pull on the protection to get across the crux traverse. This was not good. All that was needed was one truly free ascent and Everett would be happy. It had been his justification for installing all the bolts in the first place. He fretted for a while and decided he and Dave needed to bring in a ringer—a bigger gun to climb the line in better style than they could do themselves.

Jeff's friend Glenn Reisenhofer had been out of commission with a foot injury acquired in Asia, and had nothing to do with the genesis of the route. Nevertheless, after much healing and cajoling, he agreed to go up (with cane in hand) to check things out.

Reisenhofer takes over the story: "Jeff did consider employing some young sport climber to help him (he mentioned Simon Parboosingh and Rich Jagger), but it rained a lot in the spring/summer of '93, so many of our outings took place at the Back of the Lake. We were getting fairly fit and Jeff now wanted me to help him on *Gormenghast*. I think he felt badly for me, chopping off my big toe and all. Now that I was ready for action he invited me along.

"I'd never been on the route, but I was quite fit by this stage. The 2nd pitch was the crux. A relatively easy corner, 5.10ish, leads to a small roof that needs to be traversed to the left. The most difficult climbing is only ten feet long at most and it consists of a rising traverse with side pulls, one tiny edge, and very little for the feet. It took me 15 tries to free it.

"I was wasted by the time I finally got it. Luckily I got the moves, for just afterward it rained. We hung under a large roof above the crux. Everett led both the 1st and 3rd pitch while I got the 2nd and 4th pitch. He heavily sandbagged me (he's such a swine), telling me that the crux 2nd pitch was maybe 5.11 and the last pitch was around 5.10. I found that the 2nd pitch was 5.12 and the 4th pitch 5.11.

"I was a bit nervous of giving a 5.12 grade to a pitch, but I firmly felt that it was quite difficult and as other climbers have ascended the route I've asked them what they thought of the grading. Dave Crosley and Steve DeMaio climbed it together and Dave thought a 12a grade was appropriate. Tim Mooney climbed it and felt it was solid 12. Raphael Slawinski also thought it was 12a. He was disappointed that the route never went directly to the top."

So *Gormenghast* quietly became the first 5.12 climb on Yamnuska.

Anticipating sentiments like Slawinski's, Everett had hoped to add a different finish (which he intended to call "Hall of the Brilliant Carvings") that wouldn't involve *Chockstone Corner*. Reisenhofer says one

heavily overcast day Jeff set off to "inspect" the remainder of the prospective route. "He smoked a fatty and headed up to the top of the cliff. His plan was to check out the rock on the last pitch, for it looked steep and intimidating. He placed a bolt on top and planned to rap and jug on a new 10.5 mm rope and have an old 8.5 mm as a backup. In his drugged state he rapped on the ancient 8.5 mm and totally forgot about the 10.5 mm that he'd left at the top. Freaked and stoned, he now had to jug back up on his old rope with no back up. Later he joked about the incident and added that we should go back and rap-piton it."

Sweet, Safe and Straight

One of the more unheralded developments of the Nineties was the opening of *Dreambed* in 1994. This excellent line was submitted unexpectedly and seemingly out of the blue from the previously uninvolved trio of Tim Mooney, Rich Akitt and Steve Morrison. Perhaps significantly, the motivation for their climb—at least that of Mooney—was in direct response to the adventurous (read "risky") nature of many of the routes that had been established during the previous decade.

Tim Mooney. Photo Dave Dornian.

"If you do Dreambed and think you're an alpine rock climber, you're gonna be a sorry, sorry guy." (Tim Mooney)

Mooney, Akitt, and Morrison worked a total of ten days to put their climb together, a large investment of time for a route on Yam to that point. They hung from hooks and drilled by hand. Mooney says, "We—well, I did, anyway—wanted a SAFE hard route! I know Jeff [Marshall]. I know Steve. I actually climbed the first couple pitches of *Astro Yam* and felt they could have protected the climbing there better, given the methodology they used. So, I wanted to do a safer, better route."

Fairly conventionally, Tim had begun his climbing at age 16, with the Alpine Club of Canada's Calgary section. During the Eighties he had surfed a steep learning curve on Yamnuska, repeating the classics—*Forbidden Corner, CMC Wall* and *Yellow Edge*—in what he felt was good style. Then ...

"One day I went up with my girlfriend and just walked the length of the face and said, 'That's a line and there's a line, and there's a GOOD line ...' Of course, the new guidebook [Chris Perry's *Bow Valley Rock*] was out and I'd been looking at the pictures endlessly, too."

The trio's route-building efforts were episodic, as is usual with most collective enterprises on Yamnuska. The team began work in April, but it became harder and harder to return to the project as the season matured and the temperatures on the clean faces soared. "It was starting to really bake by the time we finished, later in the summer."

Using only a 9-mm rope and carrying huge packs, the group would simul-climb the adjacent *Red Shirt* route to access their high point more quickly. Mooney remembers having to grab the fraying yellow slings left by previous parties on the 2nd pitch of that route just to keep his balance and not pull the rest of the team off the mountain. "The top of *Dreambed* went in much faster, after we'd fixed the bottom of the new route with ropes."

Dreambed is known today for being one of the routes closest to a multi-pitch sport climb that Yam has to offer, requiring only a small selection of freely placed protection. However, the number and arrangement of bolts on each individual pitch varies, according to the impulse of the person who installed them. "I don't know how many bolts went in—it was the choice of who was on lead. Rich and I had some heated discussions about how close bolts should be. He was much more willing than I was to put pressure on those who would come after us. At least pitch-length occurred naturally—the ledges just showed up. The third guy would jug up with a wire brush and clean, but the rock quality was really good."

For a while there was debate and even some derision about the grade claimed for *Dreambed*. Mooney and Akitt were viewed as outsiders to the Yam scene—they had distributed topos describing the crux climbing as 5.11c, and pitches lower on the route were claimed to be only middling 5.10. The agreement today is that the key moves feel harder or easier depending on the leader's height, reach, and whether or not the 3rd pitch is climbed tight to the corner or instead attempted from the face to its left, where Mooney originally felt he had to climb to find placements for hooks from which to drill. Tim says he has returned to shoot video through the critical passages, and now agrees with others' estimations of the easier grade. He also agrees that the pitches before and after are probably quite a bit stiffer than the party initially supposed, though he has no idea how the original underrating occurred.

But more important than any hairsplitting about the size of the holds or the difficulty of individual moves, and whether or not it was recognized at the time, the appearance of *Dreambed*, coming so closely after *Gormenghast* the year before, was significant. In both cases the protagonists used their climbs to promote what they felt was a better and more considerate approach to new-routing on Yam. Mooney argues that climbs put up on such a prominent and popular crag should be built to be repeated,

that the experience of those who will inevitably follow in the future must always be borne in mind. "If you're at the belay where our route joins *Red Shirt*, you can move up and step around the corner and finish up *Jimmy and the Cruisers*. I climbed *Jimmy and the Cruisers* before I did *Dreambed*. Steve [DeMaio] didn't leave hangers on some of his bolts. I asked him about that after—he didn't give a shit."

Mooney is considerably more ambivalent about the style employed on a first ascent than are many others who have climbed on Yamnuska. He feels it is perhaps time to push through to the next level and begin installing good-quality routes on the cliff from the top down, via rappel. He'll cite others who might feel the same way, but who are perhaps reluctant to publicly step forward in the face of a vocal and high-profile minority who favour the adventure-climbing ethic. Whatever the defenders of the faith might say, he feels that the situation has reached the stage of 'why not?' He thinks people have to acknowledge that the climbing on Yamnuska has evolved to a point where it is far from a natural or unalloyed experience—"If you do *Dreambed* and think you're an alpine rock climber, you're gonna be a sorry, sorry guy."

Tim also points out that many projects on the cliff seem to go on and on under the bottom-to-top edict. He mentions the three-years-incomplete status of the Slawinski/Gadd line through the roofs to the right of *Balrog*, and his own involvement with a labour-intensive line to the right of *Astro Yam*. "There's adventure going bottom up, for the first ascensionists, but you get better quality going down. It's so much work, it's hard, bolting bottom up. I don't know if I'll ever have the time to go back there and put in the days to finish. But, yeah—I'm not going to be the one to buck the ethic."

Reisenhofer feels exactly the opposite: He says, "I must admit that I do greatly admire the bold traditional routes like *Astro Yam* and *Above and Beyond*. Why? They were

"We used to give a flying fuck who was coming up [a route] next —it was the last thing on our mind! It's a very, very different thing today. There're very few of my own routes that I'd want to go back and do again. East End Boys, yes! But not Quantum.., Or Above And Beyond." (Steve DeMaio)

"But here is how to decide what the ethic should be. First ask yourself, why do people want to have a FA on Yam? It's because having your name attached to a route and the history of the crag means something. Second question: why does it mean something? Because of the history of exploration, adventure, and ground-up development. Thus, opening the gates to rap bolting will eliminate many of the reasons people want to do a FA there in the first place."
(Joe Josephson)

put up in great style and will always be respected and viewed in awe. Can a heavily bolted climb like *Gormenghast* be respected and admired in the same fashion? No way.

"I used to clip bolts before the words 'sport climbing' existed. I can still remember when Larry Ostrander timidly used the term for the first time and it immediately caught my attention. Most climbers did both style of routes. A greater amount of experience is required to lead a route like *Astro Yam*. A huge amount of your being is placed on the sharp end. Not so for a heavily bolted climb."

Reisenhofer is adamant: "There should be one cliff that is left untouched by rap bolting. It would stain the soul of the Mother Goddess and alter the cliff forever."

Despite believing that the present self-regulation is holding back progress at the cliff, Mooney is sympathetic to Reisenhofer's argument. By not taking the current strictures too lightly, despite thinking they should be re-examined and possibly abandoned, Tim feels he is acknowledging something that is ultimately more important at the storied cliff. "Maybe it'll be me [who breaks with tradition]. More probably it'll be somebody else. However it goes, Yam will always be important not just because it can provide alpine training, and not just because it has a long season and easy access—Greenwood climbed there."

As a matter of interest, Jeff Marshall joined with the crew and did the second ascents of the Cheesmond/Quinn/Gross trilogy from 1985—*Brown Trousers, The Heat Is On*, and *The Wild Boys*—in 1994, the same year that *Dreambed* went in. Of the latter Marshall says, "That crux pitch on *Wild Boys* is INSANE! We had a sleep at the stance below it. We'd been up all night partying with Jeff Everett. Maybe that was a good thing, though—perhaps it took the edge off the situation mentally."

Coast to Coast on the Carbonate Wave

Alan Derbyshire holds the distinction of having climbed more of the routes on Yamnuska than perhaps any other person. His tally for the crag is close to 65 of the almost 100 different climbs there, depending a little bit on the definition of "different climb" and give or take a pitch or two. He's been mining the resources at the cliff ever since arriving in the area from England for the CLOD expedition to Denali in 1977. Al's first climb on Yam was an ascent of *Red Shirt* in the company of Jon Jones.

For a time Derbyshire guided Yamnuska as well as climbing there for pleasure. In the early Eighties he explored the west end of the rock, producing the disappointing *False Promise* with fellow guide Murray Toft. Although not in the forefront of the exploration boom of the late Eighties, Derbyshire visited often in the context of his work with the Lac Des Arcs Climbing School and the outdoor programs of Mount Royal College. He's the man who sent the likes of the young Jeff Everett on their first desperate encounters with Yam's classic climbs.

In 1994, Derbyshire was associated with the production of two new routes: *Hanging Out* and *Extender*. When taken together, these two climb first the face of The Tongue (a feature standing against the wall left of *Belfry*), and then the steep face and corners above. Although he put up the lower climb with Frank Campbell and the upper a short while later with Choc Quinn and Tim Auger, Al has never done the obvious thing and linked the two together into a single day's ascent. When climbed that way, in one push, they reputedly give a consistent and sustained outing at high standard, with a fair bit of 5.10 climbing and an upper crux that breaks over into the 5.11 range.

When queried about his motivation in climbing 60+ different routes on one cliff, and what might press him to constantly seek out new territory on the same small piece of geology year after year, Derbyshire is re-

Top: Alan Derbyshire. Alan Derbyshire collection.
Bottom: Alan Derbyshire. Photo Chic Scott.

luctant to sound the depths. He suspects the attraction had its beginnings in his affection for steep limestone and a fondness for traditional multi-pitch climbs, possibly developed during early visits to the Dolomites while he was still living in England. Apart from that, Yamnuska is "simply handy to the city and has lots of good routes."

Housekeeping

Around the same mid-Nineties period that *Dreambed* and *Gormenghast* were going up, there came more "sorting-out" kinds of projects on other parts of Yam. Andy Genereux teamed with American Steve Mascioli in 1995 to put up *Master Mind*, essentially a free-climbable version of *General Pain*. This was a work of rearrangement to a certain extent—the idea being to produce a cleaner, more appropriately strenuous climb. The pair began up the first three pitches of *CMC Wall* and then moved left to finish to the top of the cliff. They added a short free section over a roof and refitted the upper part of *General Pain* to allow a safer and more enjoyable outing for anyone coming after.

Whether simply housekeeping, or something more significant, *Master Mind* pointed the way to the next step for Genereux. He had dealt with all-new ground on the climb while carrying a battery-powered Hilti and drilling on lead. More work was waiting for the Bumblebee a half-kilometre further east along the cliff.

"The quality of Yam is very predictable: if there's yellowish rock on the route, be prepared to get scared, 'cause it's going to be loose. If it's grey rock, then it's excellent quality rock. Unfortunately, you still need to be prepared to get scared, 'cause there's not as much pro on the grey stuff as on the yellow stuff. Oh, and almost all the routes have some yellow stuff. Dazed and Confused even has some green stuff, which is ultra-scary." (Jeff Everett)

The East End Boy Returns

For years aspirants had speculated about—and had even inspected and attempted—a free ascent of Bill Betts' and Steve DeMaio's astonishing *East End Boys*. Simon Parboosingh made several visits in the company of Jeff Everett in the early Nineties to work out the moves to many of the difficult sections, even reportedly freeing the 3rd pitch at 5.12. Sadly, Parboosingh was killed in a mountaineering accident on Mount Athabasca before he was able to try a complete ascent of the route.

Perhaps motivated by this expressed interest by others in what had been the product of one of his best days of climbing ever, Steve DeMaio approached Andy Genereux on the tenth anniversary of the first ascent of *East End Boys* and suggested that together they tackle the problem of freeing the line.

Steve had gotten away from climbing for several years. He had worked on other projects, settled down somewhat, and pursued his career. It was Karen Snyder, Steve's new wife and an accomplished sport climber in her own right, who started him on the rock again during a vacation the two of them had taken to Thailand. Steve says, "and right away, halfway around the world, I'm thinking *East End Boys*."

On his return, DeMaio had his quiet meeting with Andy and within weeks the two were once again poking about on the climb. According to Steve, being on *East End Boys* this time around had a totally different feeling. He says he looked at some of the stances he had used on the first ascent and at the protection that had been available, and "I was thinking, 'What was I ON?!' I'd graded one pitch 5.7 A3, and I'm struggling to finish it up after the aid part, where I'd run it out, and when Andy comes up and I ask him, he says, 'That's 5.10.'"

With DeMaio returning from a climbing hiatus somewhat out of shape, the two thought some time spent on the route cleaning off dangerous holds and installing updated hardware would serve as good con-

ditioning for the free attempt. They drilled new bolts to improve the precarious old belay stances and threw down huge amounts of loose rock. All told, they took four or five days to set things up on the first five pitches.

There was a need to practice some of the harder sections, then go down to rest before returning with renewed strength for a proper continuous ascent. Genereux remembers that "Steve was trashed, because he had climbed *Bringers of the Dawn* the day before. When we went to do the complete ascent, he couldn't free the whole rig. I made him come back, again, and we finally climbed the route with NO hangs!" Ultimately, the count would rise to five tries before the pair was able to redpoint the route DeMaio had climbed with Betts in a single inspired day 11 years before.

"So Andy and I go up there to the same place 11 years later on the free attempt. I'm looking around for the wire placements. I had the drill with me and I put in another bolt. Andy arrives and looks at the stance, and looks at the overhang we have to climb. And we drill another."
(Steve DeMaio)

Steve DeMaio on the first free ascent of *East End Boys*. Photo Andy Genereux.

The Logical Extension

Genereux says he got his next idea—*Snert's Big Adventure*—from the days spent with DeMaio on *East End Boys*. ("Snert" was the nickname of Andy's most consistent partner in those days, climbing or otherwise: his dog Fergie.) The line he chose to work next that same summer of '97 was a difficult one, tracing the elegant arête that had inspired Urs Kallen and Billy Davidson's *Yellow Edge* decades previously.

> *"I think the crag mentality has to come to Yam. Like that—you can't expect to climb hard and to have things clean up just with repeats." (Andy Genereux)*

Having to begin the project by himself, Andy laboured to establish the first pitches up to an old anchor that was part of the original *Yellow Edge* aid line. Using a Rope Soloist to catch any slips, he returned alone to free the bottom three rope lengths, including the manky rivet ladder where his route crossed that of the older climb. On his fourth day up the cliff, he managed to add only a single pitch—though it ultimately proved to be the crux of the route—and came down at 10:30 pm. Dispirited by his poor progress, but still stubborn, Genereux returned a few days later, walked around to the top of the cliff, rapped in to his previous high point, and climbed the rest of the way to the top, fixing belays and establishing protection as he went.

Finally, after giving himself a week of rest (which likely included several 12 hour shifts at his regular job with the Calgary Fire Department), Andy came back to the cliff with Steve DeMaio to swing leads and the pair sent the complete line.

Below: Fergie (Snert) and Steve DeMaio at the base of *Snert's Big Adventure*. Photo Andy Genereux.

Opposite: Final pitch of *Snert's Big Adventure*. Photo Andy Genereux

How it's Done

At this point it might be appropriate to take a moment and consider the evolution of techniques employed to put up new routes on Yamnuska. Contrast, if you will, the crepe-soled street shoes and waist-tied rope favoured by Gmoser, Grillmair and party in 1952 for their first ascent of *Grillmair Chimneys* with the methodology that Andy and others have developed for establishing modern routes today.

From the very beginning there has been a sentiment expressed that a new route on Yamnuska should be climbed from the bottom of the cliff to its upper edge, with the leader approaching each rope length of a first ascent without prior knowledge of the holds or ledges that might be above. Although this tactic may seem self-evident to the uninitiated, traditional methods are by no means the only way of establishing a new route on a cliff like Yam. On a mountain where school classes shod only in running shoes can scramble easily around either end of the cliff and up its gentle back slopes to the summit, there is a strong temptation for more ambitious climbers to throw gear and ropes into a pack and do the same. Once on the upper rim of the cliff, the line of a prospective route might be inspected from the relative safety of a series of rappels down the face. Loose rock could be thrown off, the easiest path of ascent could be determined, and any needed hardware or permanent means of protection could be installed prior to an actual attempt to "lead" a climb.

Thus, as far as credit for a first ascent on Yamnuska goes, the most efficient approach is argued to comprise unfair tactics. The claim is made that working top down shortcuts a necessary sense of adventure, and removes that certain thrill of exploration true first ascensionists are expected to face. Whereas with other pursuits—a novelist, say, might be permitted to decide the ending of his book before beginning the first chapter, or a film director allowed to shoot a movie out of the order in which it will play—a new rock climb on Yamnuska is expected to be developed sequentially. Most feel a climb put up on the cliff today should be introduced in the same spirit, if not exactly the same manner, as essayed 50 years ago—each fresh expanse of stone to be approached for the first time from below, with climbers then proceeding upward through the unknown until there is nothing left but the sky.

Unlike those pioneers, however, modern high-standard rock climbers are desirous of moving their efforts out onto the blank faces and away from the cracks and corners followed (of necessity) by climbers from previous generations. To this end, today's activists have elaborated on the tactics first employed with the ascent of *Astro Yam*. Although climbers attempting a new route will initiate each rope length of climbing from below, and place any anchors as they climb upward, the tendency now is to work with the convenience and safety of future climbers in mind. Protection from expansion bolts is arranged wherever there are no options for placing removable anchors. To ensure that these permanent bits of hardware are installed to specification, a cordless masonry drill such as the Hilti TE10A is carried on a shoulder bandolier or chest harness. Such a device weighs over five kilos with its large battery pack (often connected in series to obtain more power) and adds considerably to the encumbrance of the leader. In the event of a mishap the drill bit extending from the tool's business end can present a significant hazard.

So starting out below a new stretch of rock, the climber will array himself or herself with the hardware they think might be needed on the pitch to come. This can constitute quite a load, and might include the drill, a hammer for driving bolts, a wrench for nuts and capscrews, some sort of device for blowing the dust out of freshly drilled holes, possibly a chisel for levelling the surface of the rock where a bolt will be placed, etc. Additionally, two adjustable leashes, each attached to a small, hard steel hook, are sometimes tied to the front of the climber's harness.

Struggling upward into the unknown with all this extra kit swaying and banging can be quite an experience! Trying to plan for difficult sequences of moves as the climbing proceeds, the leader might elect to place a bolt if there is no alternative for something more convenient. As soon as this decision has been taken, he or she will seek a position from which to stand and drill, since two hands are best for the task. Typically, however, the reason the bolt is needed in the first place is to protect climbing over ground that is either very steep or very difficult or both, often presenting only small, widely spaced holds. The first alternative when both hands cannot be lowered at once, if our leader is trying to free the pitch, is to cling to a good hold and work one-handed. This can be massively strenuous, but is possible under the right circumstances.

If the one-handed approach doesn't prove feasible, the next choice of tactic is to give in to the difficulty of the climbing and acknowledge that your party will have to return and climb the pitch free at another time, whereupon the leader can relent and engineer direct support from either conventional climbing hardware like pitons, camming devices, or chocks, or drop a hook on some convenient edge or tuck it behind a little flake before hanging to drill and install a bolt and hanger. Of course, just as soon as anything but the rock itself has been weighted, the free climbing has ended and the attempt has reverted to what is called an "aided" ascent.

This is NOT to say that the enterprise suddenly becomes easy once a decision to hang has been made. Eldon Formation limestone being the variable medium that it is, drilling from hooks is far from simple *or* safe. Placements can easily skate off ledges that are pitched at less than right angles to the direction a dangling climber might pull on them. While swinging about attempting to bring power tools into play, a few taps with a hammer can set the points of a hook into the soft carbonate in order to prevent shifting, but judgment is required here as well—

Andy Genereux drilling on *Master Mind*.
Photo Steve Mascioli.

striking with too much nervous enthusiasm will change the nature of the climbing itself, leaving ugly scars and possibly creating (or destroying) a hand or foothold. Moreover, the entire placement could "blow." Far and away the greatest terror associated with the entire operation is having the rock itself calve from the face under the immense pressure exerted on the tiny area where the hook contacts the stone. The points on a skyhook are chisel sharp at the contact surface, and might be narrower than a screwdriver blade. Hang from that an 85 kg climber shouldering another 10 kg of gear and rope. Then have her or him bounce up and down and hammer at the rock. The forces generated at the tip of the hook can be high enough to fuse diamonds. It's a lot to expect a small edge of calcite to withstand without exploding.

If the hooks do hold, and the rock holds too, the drill is brought into play and a precise hole is placed where it is estimated that an unencumbered leader on some later ascent would most like to clip a piece of protection as he passes. The drill bit is withdrawn from the hole—careful, it's hot enough to melt synthetic fabrics—dust is cleared by blowing through a tube, and a bolt is selected, inserted, and driven home with the hammer. A hanger is placed over the shaft of the bolt, and then a cap screw or nut is applied to the threads and torqued with a wrench to the proper tension. Only then is the anchor ready to have a carabiner hung from it and the climber's rope clipped through it for safety. The entire process can be a laborious one, often made desperate by duress. Over the years virtually all of the new-route protagonists on Yamnuska—including Brian Gross, Steve DeMaio, Joe Josephson, and Jeff Marshall, as well as Andy Genereux—have taken serious falls while struggling to place protection by this means on their climbs.

To return to Genereux specifically, Andy often compounds the difficulty of putting up routes by working alone ("cell phones are great," he says), self-belaying with a device called a Soloist while he cleans loose rock and figures out a climb. This not only prevents partner burnout while Andy works long hours to put a pitch together, but also suits his personality and professional schedule. However, being high on the mountain by himself also brings greater risk of accident or injury. A hundred metres up the side of a cliff like Yamnuska definitely qualifies as a hazardous environment. The consequences of making a mistake while by yourself on the face could be quite serious.

> *"Andy often compounds the difficulty of putting up routes by working alone."*

Super SDAG

When asked about his latest projects and future ambitions on Yamnuska, Genereux waxes enthusiastic. In the latter Nineties, together with Steve DeMaio and Joe Josephson he began work on a line to the right of *CMC Wall* and by the end of '98 had completed the first couple of pitches. However, Josephson's move to the U.S., and DeMaio's growing commitment to work and family, slowed the project to the point where they were unable to finish until 2001. Though he was returning, fit, to Yamnuska soon after their *East End Boys* reprise, DeMaio suffered an asthma attack on his and Andy's second or third attempt and essentially retired again. Genereux spent more than a year incapacitated by a series of back surgeries. In the end DeMaio waited until Andy was ready, and let him lead all of the new ground on their intended route.

Even with its multi-year schedule the outcome was never certain. During one of the final efforts a homebuilt battery rig that Andy had designed to carry in a backpack malfunctioned and began to burn through his shirt, giving him a "hot back." It was day five (and year four) on the climb, and impatience lent him the strength to shed the offending gear and place bolts through the crux moves with a hand drill. The two returned again, but were forced to finish up *CMC Wall*. One week later, Genereux came back alone, in bad weather, to rap in from the top of *CMC Wall*. He climbed out to the rim once more by a truly new pitch, thus creating a fully independent route: *Super SDAG* (Super Direct Adventure with Gravity). Genereux claims he was just trying to compose an anagram that employed Steve and his initials to describe this good climb.

Records and Roadmaps

Unlike many of Yamnuska's homeboys, Joe Josephson did not grow up within school-field-trip range of the Bow Valley climbing areas. Rather, he travelled to Calgary in 1988 from his family home in Montana to enroll in the Faculty of Outdoor Pursuits at the University of Calgary (ODPU). Like a new chum finding the bad part of town, he began to hang around The Wildboys climbing shop on 4th Street. As if that wasn't enough, Josephson also came to frequent the Calgary Mountain Club's slide shows on Wednesday nights in the low-rent bars downtown. He gradually made friends with many of the members.

Still shy, though, most of Josephson's early climbing in the Calgary region happened in the company of fellow students Stephen Ritchie, Brian Spear and Jeff Nazarchuk. Unlike many others who came to the cliff for their initiation, Joe was, in his words, "...climbing a ton, so when I got to Yam I was already up on that alpiny stuff." Yamnuska suited Joe's sensibilities, and once introduced to the situation on the cliff, he "pretty much climbed up there continuously."

Despite his mountain experience, Josephson still had neophyte moments. During an early encounter with Steve DeMaio, he found himself committed to a day's climbing on the route that would eventually become *Jimmy and the Cruisers*. During their hike up to the base of the rock and the walk along the face, DeMaio regaled the young Joe with horror stories about the climbing on *East End Boys*. "Then, PSHEW! He's gone up the hill. When I catch up, he looks at me with those huge eyes, and says, 'The key to today ... is speed!' I was just belaying. And he's making me take his hangers off and I'm struggling. It was way over my head at the time. The next time we were out, Steve went back on his route with Jeff Nazarchuk. I just went down the cliff and did *Pangolin*. I was much happier with myself, then."

Joe Josephson racking up for *Smeagol*.
Photo Pat Morrow.

"...he pieced the idea of the radical line together. He knew it would make both a beautiful and a difficult climb. He also realized it would be much work ... and then had to face the question 'WHO do I get to go up on this with me?'"

In the years immediately following (the early Nineties), Josephson was distracted from Yamnuska by similar walls in the Ghost River valleys to the north. It was in that huge and underdeveloped arena that the ever-active Andy Genereux impressed Josephson with the potential of carrying a Hilti power drill while on lead. The two worked on a number of projects together, and Joe says, "I began to feel like I had an eye for a line, with climbs like *Zephyr*, there."

Reconnecting with his pal Brian Spear and a number of other friends, Joe returned to Yamnuska and contributed to the production of *Gargoyle* in 1996, then helped Spear begin a route that would ultimately become 2001's *Boomerang*. Both of these climbs worked through the steep, confused geometry at the far east end of the mountain, long-neglected because of the perception that the rock on that part of the cliff was of poorer quality. Also, the slightly lower elevation of the wall there was felt to be less worthy of attention.

Joe was pleased with both the experience and the results of their efforts. "I was really inspired by the style—it was a cool blending of methods [using a power drill on lead] that preserved the adventure of the exploration. Climbing off and on with DeMaio, I'd got lots of stories, and an insight into the adventure ethic up there."

To hear the story told, however, and to climb that same story, are different levels of experience. Josephson is quick to reveal that an early repeat of the seminal *The Heat Is On* in the company of Tim Auger was something of a revelation. "We had one rope. Four pitons. NO hammer! And we DO it! I remember sitting belaying Tim on the crux pitch and thinking, 'we can't go down.' For the first time up there, I was cut off and just having fun. Tim, he told me stories that day about climbing *Kahl Wall* with Vockeroth."

Joe claims he was similarly inspired by climbing *Yellow Edge* with Tim Pochay, and getting out with Brian Gross onto *CMC Wall*.

Starving writers camped in Yam meadows. Chic Scott was working on *Pushing the Limits* and Joe Josephson on *Bow Valley Rock*. Photo Chic Scott collection.

A year earlier, back with Barry Blanchard from an attempt on Logan "where all we did was shovel snow," the two headed up to Yamnuska for sun and an ascent of *Mum's Tears*. For whatever reason they deviated toward better rock they thought they could see to the right of *Necromancer* that day, and quickly produced a route they frivolously called *Mexican Backhoe*.

More importantly, a few weeks later in that same summer of '95, Josephson and Blanchard played host to high-profile visitors Jay Smith and Kitty Calhoun on *Kahl Wall*. The two were pointing things out to the Americans. Looking around, and then down from the ledge mid-route, Joe saw a line of holds leading across a beautiful gray slab. Going back and examining that part of the cliff over further trips, he pieced the idea of the radical line together. He knew it would make both a beautiful and a difficult climb. He also realized it would be much work … and then had to face the question "WHO do I get to go up on this with me?"

In the early season of 1996, Jeff Everett and Dave Campbell climbed the hilariously eccentric *Jazz Beat of the Nun's Groove*. Their line wandered all over the rock between *Unnamed* route and *Missionary's Crack*. As an experiment, Everett celebrated the ascent by writing his description of the route while drunk, in an imitation of Jack Kerouac's beat style. Not surprisingly, the earnest *Canadian Alpine Journal* rejected the article. According to Everett, a drugged hospital patient suggested the name for the climb, and Jeff's written version of the story featured driving, hitchhikers, loud music, playing cards, cheap red wine, a silk jacket, and of course a nun. Somehow the story suited the erratic, rambling nature of the route.

That same spring Jojo's big question was answered. He enticed a weekday climbing accomplice for the project he'd envisioned the year before, albeit a partner who made for one of the more unlikely match-ups on the crag. He had cold-called Shep Steiner,

Jeff Everett on *Jazz Beat of the Nun's Groove*.
Photo Dave Campbell

Jazz Beat of the Nun's Groove. Photo Glenn Reisenhofer.

"Bringers was, like, a fun route to do—I can't even remember much about it except that the climbing was great! We managed to do about a pitch and a half a day. It was exciting even if we weren't so efficient! We'd be up there doing stuff like throwing to little edges and then trying to put down a hook, Andy Genereux style. It'll never be so adventurous for any later ascent party." (Shep Steiner)

met once up at the cliff where he was working on his own project. This act must have taken a little bit of courage right from the start, for Steiner enjoyed a reputation as a longtime mountain bum and perennial art student notorious for his flamboyant personality and headlong climbing style. In the Banff/Canmore community Steiner was legendary for his impulsiveness and extreme confidence—surely the polar opposite of Josephson's sensitive personality. But amazingly, the two shared a love of Yamnuska climbing at a time when most climbers in the area were involved with sport climbing or other mountains. They hit it off immediately. Josephson says, "It was cool. Shep told me these great stories about *Verstiegenheit* [an extreme line that is still a project of Steiner's today, left of *Master Mind* and *CMC Wall*] ...and he'd done, like, the second ascent of *Freak Out.*"

The pair was uncertain what others would think about their tactic of using the power drill on Yamnuska. Though they were working bottom-up, and drilling their bolts on lead, most (though not all) work on new routes up to that point had relied on hand drills, a somewhat self-limiting strategy.

On their first go at the proposed line, Josephson ran out of battery power and had to traverse far left to where he could set a natural anchor. They rapped. Returning, they retraced the route and Steiner put in pitch 4. Josephson installed the hardware on pitch 5 and once again they bailed for the valley. When they came back, their finishing kick was to be a little more controversial in style—they walked around the end of the cliff and hiked up to the top of their intended route, rappelled down to their previous high point, and installed the needed fixed protection through to pitch 7.

Opposite: Shep Steiner starting the 5.11 climbing on pitch 2, *Bringers of the Dawn.* Photo Joe Josephson.

Shep Steiner and Hilti on *Bringers of the Dawn*, *Kahl Wall* behind. Photo Joe Josephson.

The tactics became even more convoluted as the pair attempted to complete the task. Because of the way they had been approaching the climbing—bottom up, but starting in different places—there was also some question in their minds about just what might constitute a finish to the climbing. The next time they walked up the hill, they ascended what is now the 1st pitch [they had been scrambling to the top of this feature from the left, as if beginning *Kahl Wall*]. Then they came down, walked around to the top of the cliff again and rappelled all the way down, adjusting and "messing around." On this top-to-bottom pass Shep top-roped pitch 6 successfully. As Joe says, "At that point we'd done them all."

Looking for a complete, bottom-to-top ascent in the classic style, however, the two went back on the route later during that fall

of '96 and "failed miserably, both falling." It wasn't until the following spring, in 1997, that the two managed to find the time and the conditions to get together and finally send *Bringers of the Dawn* cleanly, leading each pitch without falls.

Josephson suggests that the arduous schedule for *Bringers* wasn't necessarily a matter of that route's difficulty alone. He good-humouredly suspects Steiner of hidden agendas—taking advantage of the pair's necessary repeat trips to the mountain to dragoon assistance for attempts on his other project. "We'd be fully doing this heinous alpine rap epic, just so Shep could drop in at the end of a long day to top rope a couple of pitches on *Verstiegenheit*." But Josephson acknowledges the debt *Bringers of the Dawn* owes to Steiner's free-climbing energy and prowess. "On the final go on *Bringers*, Shep led the 7th pitch for me because I was afraid I'd blow it and we'd have to come back AGAIN."

The ice had been broken with *Bringers*, at least in Jojo's mind, and similar piecework tactics were employed the following season when he linked sections of *Kahl Wall*, *Trap Line*, and *Forbidden Corner* with only a few pitches of excellent new climbing to create *The Milky Way*—a name suggested by Steiner. It ascends an arching band of grey rock that sweeps across the centre of the face and is the longest route on the cliff.

Josephson enlisted a number of partners, primarily Dave Dornian, to help him link the climbing and clean the line. To access the widely separate portions of the route, the protagonists would usually climb in from an already established adjacent line, or rappel down *Forbidden Corner* to get on the upper pitches.

And it was here, on the second to last pitch, that Dornian discovered one of the small but abiding mysteries of Yamnuska. Working with a Hilti while on lead, Dave had climbed and traversed more than 20 metres of tricky moves that would ultimately be graded 5.9+. He had eased his

Joe Josephson on the final pitch of *The Milky Way*. Photo Pat Morrow.

Dave Dornian. Photo Maja Swannie.

Dave Dornian, Joe Josephson and Tim Auger in the Yam parking lot, 1997. Photo Dave Dornian.

mind by placing several pieces of modern protection and had drilled three bolts to secure blank passages along the way—all before he encountered an ancient angle piton hammered in a shallow corner. Although there was no further evidence of a previous ascent to be found, it can only be presumed that this mysterious relic belonged to an early exploration toward the top of *Forbidden Corner*. If indeed the rusting piton belonged to Don Vockeroth, or to Lloyd MacKay, or to a contemporary (Urs Kallen suggests it was placed by the late George Homer), then it would have marked a line climbed at a time when there were no bolts or chocks or modern camming devices. As Josephson, already steeped in the lore of the cliff at that time, said later, "We are not worthy."

Once again it was some time before disparate schedules would allow a continuous ascent, but the route was complete and saw several ascents before the end of the 1998 season.

Although he was managing to add new routes to the cliff at the rate of approximately one per year during this period, Josephson was perpetually at the crag, climbing anything and everything he could find partners for. He had ideas for many other new routes and variations, and began work on several of them with different accomplices. As an example, he helped Steve DeMaio with the starting pitches of a new line to the right of *CMC Wall* (that would eventually become *Super SDAG* in 2001), but felt "that was like, one of ten I was trying to prioritize."

Being unable to keep involved in the first ascents of all the good projects he'd envisioned did not dismay Josephson. Speaking on the telephone from Montana, he still avers that "if someone goes and does one of the routes I've had my eyes on, I'm psyched. I learned that from Steve, actually watching and listening to him get news from others in the bar, at the Drake in Canmore, after climbing one day."

During this time Josephson formalized his love of Yamnuska by agreeing to compile and write the long-needed update that was planned for the new edition of *Bow Valley Rock*. "I was trying to tick 50 routes on the cliff. I was fully into the guidebook at the time. I had all this stuff going on in my life, too, and I wanted to do a GOOD job. Drawing good topos of the routes up there for the first time ever. Topos are really challenging up there on Yam."

The sense of custodial duty doesn't end for Josephson with the current completion of his portion of the Bow Valley guidebook —"I love telling stories and discussing things with people on the way up to the crag. It's one of my favourite things about climbing there."

Josephson enjoys not only the place, but also the people and the culture surrounding the climbing on Yamnuska. He'll circle back through a conversation and say something like, "I think Andy, Shep, Jeff, and Keith need to be called on the carpet for all the *Astro Yam* stuff," referring to the long-dormant controversy surrounding the alleged grading of the crux pitches during early repeat ascents. Then he'll add something like, "Shep was totally respectful of the achievement there. Did you know that he fell on the crux pitch there? Yeah, and then he stopped on a ledge rather than coming back to the belay, UNTIED, and pulled the rope down and retied, all at this little teetering rest!" Or "One of the coolest things ever, that nobody mentions, is [Geoff] Powter trying to climb *Yellow Edge*—Geoff went up there with Anne Ryall, gets lost, and ON-SIGHTS the rivet ladder. Years after the first free ascent of the line was 'stolen' by Zach [Colin Zacharias] and [Peter] Croft. I think that's so cool!"

Celebrating CMC Wall

Urs Kallen, who'd spent years in the early Seventies working and then finally winning the first ascent of *CMC Wall* with Billy Davidson—Kallen, who in the prime of his climbing career had needed a desperate two days to climb out to the top of the cliff at a hideous grade of A4—walked into Mountain Equipment Co-op one day in 1997 and chatted with Jeff Marshall. As he tells it, "I said, 'Jeff, we've got to go do *CMC Wall*—it will be twenty-five years.'"

Though Urs suspects Marshall was a little surprised, Jeff agreed, and Kallen trained. Urs climbed the *Beckey/Chouinard* on South Howser Tower in the Bugaboos. Then he trained even more. Typically, this exercise took the form of long Monday evenings on the greasy concrete cracks of the University of Calgary's climbing pit. Then the two men reclimbed *CMC Wall*, free and in the modern style, on June 20, 1997.

Jeff Marshall and Urs Kallen celebrating Urs' 25th anniversary ascent of *CMC Wall*. Photo Urs Kallen collection.

Into 2000
Young Men—Old Style

"Yam tops them all because everybody's left their mark on Yam." (Chris Perry)

Left to right: Dave Crosley, Dion Bretzloff, Ben Firth, Jim Racette. Photo Ben Firth collection.

Ben Firth. Photo Ben Firth collection.

Something that becomes increasingly common, now that a half-century of history has flickered like an old film across the screen of Yamnuska, is the second-generation climber. Ben Firth is the son of Jack Firth, a longtime member of the Calgary Mountain Club who was firmly on the cutting edge of the Rockies scene throughout the 1970s.

Living in Canmore, son Ben grew up among climbers, with the activists of the day often in his house. Ben remembers listening to the likes of Chris Perry over the family dining table at home. He was impressed by the stories he heard, and maintains he was even more affected by the sense of respect the adults had for the mountain and the place it held in regional climbing history. "I kind of looked on it as a place to make a mark. Choc Quinn, Dave Cheesmond ... I was fully aware of that. All that tradition."

Firth credits this environment for his development and style preferences. He believes he picked up an appreciation of traditional rock climbing from his father. Either that, or he inherited Jack's stubbornly rebellious attitude. However it happened, Ben is the most prominent of a small number of youthful, ambitious climbers who were significantly active on Yamnuska during the late Nineties.

He recalls starting climbing on Yam when he was 13 or 14 years old, most likely in the company of his dad. With little more introduction than that, Firth went on with a handful of friends from school to venture repeatedly onto routes whose fearsome reputation had repelled suitors since a time before he was born. Ben describes how he read the guides and researched his father's book collection and "did the trade routes like *Forbidden Corner*. But then I just jumped to the hard routes. I haven't even done *CMC Wall*."

During the period around 1996 and '97, in combination with a variety of partners from the new, aggressive generation that was emerging in the Bow Valley, he freed long-standing stretches of aid on Yam's routes, and revisited scary, seldom-contemplated

Dave Crosley and Ben Firth in parking lot before the FFA of *Trap Line.* Photo Joe Josephson.

mysteries from the previous decade. The more difficult a Yamnuska test piece, the more it attracted him directly, he says.

"Me and Dave [Crosley] skipped school to go on *Corkscrew.* I had maybe asked Chris about it, about the bolt ladder and everything, when he was over at my dad's. So, we were up there and like, Dave was getting all riled up. It wasn't just school. We both had jobs at Marra's [a grocery store in Canmore] that we had to get back to."

It had taken them a number of attempts, and more than a little nerve for Ben to climb away from the old hardware along a line where only a few marginal holds could be found.

In the end the boys were two hours late for work, but they had finished the route and the overhanging ladder of old bolts that had been used for artificial aid since the first ascent 29 years before had gone free. What could be reported when the two met Barry Blanchard on their way off the hill was the accomplishment of what was possibly the most difficult stretch of free climbing on Yam. It was May of 1996.

The year was far from over for Firth and for the powerful and ever-steady Crosley. The pair also repeated *The Quickening* ("a garbage route—terrible!"), and freed *Marriage Rites* before the season was done. On the latter outing they shared a rope with Paul Valiulis.

145

Marriage Rites, Firth feels, is one of the more exceptional routes on the mountain. "Three stars—that is a classic line, man! But I don't think anybody's done that route—the bolts the guidebook says are at the end of the traverse were gone—pulled, with only one left, rusted!"

In 1997 the pair were back to establish an unaided *Trap Line*. "Dave freed the bolts—I couldn't believe how calm he was, and the effort—I was terrified for him. Then we rapped. Fuckin' typical Steve [DeMaio], he takes his hangers off! Dave gets there and does a really good job. I was shitting my pants on our complete go. Then, like meeting Blanchard after *Corkscrew*, we saw Joe [Josephson] and Steve when we came down." Firth giggles. "We found a live snake on the road and put it in the register box by the road barrier for them to find. To this day they deny seeing it!

"Basically, the whole thing [pushing to repeat the 'hard' routes] started with *Astro Yam*—doing that with Dave. Trevor Jones was over on *Direttissima*, egging us on. Jim [Racette] leant back on the extra bolt that Simon [Parsons] had drilled [on the 3rd ascent], and the cap broke off! Sure, we were scared, and later we were scared on all the other repeats, but what I learned there… was not to be intimidated by reputations.

"No offense to those guys, but they didn't know how to drill. We were prepared for the missing hangers after *Trap Line*. I got in the habit of taking along a hand drill to beef up the belays."

In 1997 the crew chose to repeat the definitive *Above and Beyond*. On their first attempt Firth went on the route with Sean Isaac and Racette. He pulled a rock loose and it hit Jim, causing a wound that would ultimately require 20 stitches to close. Ben was far out on lead when the incident happened, in a very exposed position. The two at the belay below were bleeding and screaming. Firth, reluctant to rely on the bad single bolt that was all that was available, climbed back and forth searching for gear placements before he could lower off and the team could retreat.

Racette and Firth returned two or three months later, but on this occasion managed to get lost and waste enough daylight to force them down again. Finally, on their third attempt, the party finished to the top of the route at 1 am. It was pitch black and the trio had no lights. They crawled on their hands and knees down the back of the mountain.

Ben feels that the repeats by the Canmore crowd during the later Nineties did nothing to blunt the edge or detract from the reputation of the big climbs on Yamnuska. Despite climbing routes at the highest technical standards, he says, "They were all tough for me. Some days it's the hardest thing, just to step off the belay on a 5.8!"

When queried about the place that Yamnuska holds in his climbing world now, Ben is candid, saying "To tell you the truth, I haven't climbed a lot on Yam in the past three years. Dave hasn't been up there in a while, either." But he adds, quickly "I love the ethic there. We're talking about the ground-up stuff —I think that's good 'cause it'll prolong route development. It's got a bit of that grit thing. Climbing on Yam is a transition between alpine and cragging. Just look at who has been big up there."

Ben believes Yamnuska is both a place to train and a place to prove oneself. As for the future, and what might come next on the cliff, Firth is considering picking up some of the challenges cast down by the likes of Marshall, and working toward speed ascents and multi-route enchainments.

He's also keen on new lines, and believes the rock on Yamnuska is far from fully exploited. He claims he'd like to have a look at "that headwall left of *East End Boys*—you'd take big air working that one out, but …"

Opposite: Eammon Walsh and Stephen Holeczi on *Astro Yam*, 2001. Photo Ben Firth.

Peter Gatzsch and Urs Kallen on top of Yamnuska.
Photo Urs Kallen collection.

The Bolt Nazi

Urs had spotted the start for the route years before he actually tied in below it.

Despite the passage of time and the demands of work and family, Urs Kallen always has a list of potential lines at hand—things he's seen from other routes, features on the face that show only in certain light or at particular times of day. And he wants to see these climbed.

Just as an aside: go ahead—look the man up and ask. He will happily share his hoard of information. And he'll tell you what you need to know to get started.

Anyway, *The Bolt Nazi* … Urs saw the start, and looked at the blocky overhangs higher up beneath the bolts on *Corkscrew*. He knew it was the best rock on Yam, but would it go free?

In 1999, Urs and Peter Gatzsch, after examining their intended line from the neighbouring *Corkscrew*, climbed the lower V-groove of the new route. Directly above that, Peter led through an overhanging layback. Then they climbed the bolts on *Corkscrew*, crossing that route, and headed straight up the grey wall above. Next time on the rock, the pair climbed up *Corkscrew*, through the bolt ladder, and lowered onto the ledge below, midway up the new line. Peter put in five or six new bolts. They finished up *Cork-*

screw that day, but climbed their new last pitch, and "NOW THERE'S A BOLT THERE! And chalk marks…"

The third time up the hill they managed the whole thing, with Peter climbing the bolt ladder free. "He fell off a couple of times. Saw nice air," Kallen says. The two then climbed two pitches straight up, with the second having no fixed gear, and rejoined *Corkscrew* at that route's final belay.

"The reason I called it *The Bolt Nazi* is because when Trevor [Jones] and Blob [Wyvill] went to do the second ascent they got on the route, and Blob is putting in bolts … Blob of all people—he knows. He is always talking about other people's bolts and here he is putting bolts in on OUR route. And I'm already annoyed about the bolt that showed up higher up and I'm sort of thinking of Seinfeld—I just saw the television show with the Soup Nazi episode—and I said, 'They're a bunch of bolt Nazis.' [Trevor responds in protest that he and Blob were only "beefing up the station" prior to retreating, though "we DO recommend a couple more bolts!"]

"That's how the route got the name. Later, Raphael [Slawinski] graded it 5.11b or c. I could just follow it. Putting a bolt in will kill Peter's brilliant lead."

Family Man

Steve DeMaio laughs about the future—his future. As far as plans for climbing on Yamnuska go, he still has a couple of projects left incomplete on the cliff, climbs he has been involved with to a greater or lesser extent in recent years. But he's uncertain about his motivation or potential to complete the routes in the style in which he would like to see them done. "I have one unfinished project between *East End Boys* and *Jimmy and the Kid* that I started with Naz [Jeff Nazarchuk] and Ken Wylie. I continued a bit with Ben [Firth] and Dave [Crosley]—they freed the first two pitches, I added one, and that's how it's stood now for four years. What do I do? Those guys are fucking superheroes now, and they're wanting to go back and finish up!

"I backed off a lot of routes on Yam last year. Choc and I came down from *Jimmy and the Cruisers*—we turned around 50 feet from the top. I wear my seat belt all the time [in the car] since Steph [Steve and Karen's new daughter] was born. The hunger is gone. The stakes are just too high."

Performance Art

When they speak of Yamnuska's future, it's easy to understand why climber after climber offers Shep Steiner as a fountain of positive energy, and cites him as a wellspring of motivation they can return to again and again.

It's June 18, 2002. Shep Steiner is just down from an ascent of *Snert's Big Adventure* and is raving over the telephone about the quality of the climbing. "It's a great, great route! You gotta do it! It's, like, wide-open climbing. Not like *Yellow Edge*. I think the 2nd pitch is the hardest! The 1st is a little more pumping." The topic swerves abruptly and the next thing Steiner asks about is if Andy Genereux and Urs Kallen have finished a route they were working on near the east end of the cliff. Then he describes hearing Andy (he says he *thinks* it was Andy's voice) shouting and swear-ing at a hiker on the hillside below the route. And right after that he's off on a different tangent, talking about dogs a little bit, and after that running through the sequence of moves leading up to and past the point where he fell on *Snert's*, with a voice so enthusiastic you can see him pawing at the air and waving his hands at the other end of the telephone connection. "I was SO PUMPED, and I, like, stabbed my foot on this little highstep... and chucked!"

Winding down only a little, he relates how he's planning to climb *Master Mind* on the coming weekend, and outlines his intent to use that route to connect to the upper pitches of his project, *Verstiegenheit,* "for a little more practice."

Steiner wasn't directly involved on any new projects on Yamnuska for ten years following the *Astro Yam* episode of the mid-Eighties, choosing instead to focus most of his new-route energies on high-standard sport climbs throughout the rest of the Bow Valley. In 1997, however, he revisited the cliff. During a break from the episodic but almost endless university education that had him attending Simon Fraser University on the Lower Mainland, Shep hooked up with Steve Lubnic and the two divined, cleaned and hand-drilled the necessary bolts on the first five pitches of a visionary line soaring up to the left of *General Pain*. This act was to define the project that would become something of a nemesis during his visits to the cliff in the years that followed. The idea—the climb—quickly came to be called *Verstiegenheit,* which was Shep's way of acknowledging the Austrian heritage grounding the history of Yamnuska. It was also a crib from his academic involvement in aesthetics and existentialist philosophy. Roughly characterized, the term refers to 'the state of mind of climbing too high', with the subtext being 'and not being able to come back to the ground'. The route as it stands overhangs so much that climbers retreating after a failed attempt must bounce strenuously out from the wall while they are rappelling just so that they might swing in far enough to snag the next lower station on the way down.

Todd Guyn. Photo Shep Steiner.

"There's a serious fear factor on *Verstiegen-heit*. It's so pumpy, and the rock isn't the best. It is going to be the hardest thing on Yam. The tentative grades suggested in the guidebook are low—the 2nd pitch is going to be, like, 12b, then 12 minus, then another 12. And it's going to be SO out there! So, yeah, probably one, two, three, four pitches of 12, with one pitch of 5.13 in the middle! A micro-edge sequence finishing with a dyno, then overhanging 5.11 the rest of the way."

Talented Canmore climber Todd Guyn has been Shep's most consistent partner on the *Verstiegenheit* project over the years since its conception. Together they linked the first four pitches in 2001, cleanly climbing all the moves. However, the climb remains uncompleted. Below the 5th pitch the pair traversed right and finished up *CMC Wall* to the top of the cliff. Shep says that

he began to install the hardware on the upper pitches while on rappel and missed the proper positioning of the bolts as a result. The difficulties there remain, waiting to be sorted out and climbed properly. Further work needs to be done as well to reposition the protection for a legitimate attempt to lead the upper sections free.

So today the climb still stands incomplete—desperately hard, awesomely run-out, and intimidating as hell. All but one of the pitches have been freed at one time or another, but a continuous ascent of *Verstiegenheit* lies in the indefinite future. The task looms in Steiner's mind. "It takes Todd and I a couple of days just to lose the shakes after being up there."

Sometimes it takes longer. In the fall of 2002, on yet another penultimate redpoint attempt, Guyn suffered a long, battering fall that was extended even further when he became unclipped from a bolt. He finished by crashing heavily against the wall below Steiner before he was caught on the rope. Todd was hurt enough by the impact, and Shep was alarmed enough, that they retreated from the route for the season, bruised and beaten once again.

Guyn is taciturn: "The horrible thing is, the route's not that good. The rock is hideous! The moves are low percentage." Yet Steiner is undaunted. He will casually admit defeat in conversation, then spin off toward something totally unrelated: "Hey, did you hear? Did you know there was a full accident off the 7th pitch of *Forbidden Corner* on Saturday? We think the guy broke his leg. We heard a guy shouting, 'Can anybody hear us?' during a quiet moment as we were heading down the hill. Called in a helicopter rescue. They flew, like, 20 parks staff up to the top of the cliff above the victim. They all wanted to have their finger in the pie.

"And Andy shouting at the tourists was because they were trying to steal his dog while he was up on his project. They thought a cruel person had tied her up and left her!" He laughs.

For Everyman's Climbing

Sometimes an activist's reasons for climbing revolve around complex personality issues. A few feel a need for risk and recognition. Others take climbing as an opportunity to prove themselves to themselves, or to their friends, or as an outlet for their antagonism and anger toward the restrictive "civilised" world. Not so Brian Spear.

He argues that he is a pilgrim—a member of the congregation who attends regularly for the simple pleasure of repeating outstanding mid-standard routes, immersed in the special pleasure of doing familiar things.

Like a number of others, Spear makes part of his living as an ACMG climbing guide by introducing clients to the classic Yamnuska experience. He will escort parties on the mountain "maybe 20 days a year. Mostly on the west end, or on *Direttissima*. I frame that one heavily as a big adventure, which it is."

On the way to or from a chosen climb, or on the route itself, Spear will tell the stories of the first ascents of *Grillmair Chimneys*, *Unnamed*, or *Calgary Route*, sharing the lore and legends of the front ranges' most important cliff with an ever-widening circle of devotees.

"*Missionary's!* Just think of Vockeroth! You know, I would sit on a ledge and think about those guys and what it would be like. I remember being on a ledge at the top of *Forbidden Corner* looking around and wondering 'if I didn't know where to go, where would I go?'"

In 1996 Spear and Josephson put up *Gargoyle*. Josephson took a good "whipper", in Spear's words, when he blew a hook while drilling. Then later on they came under serious fire from a group of school children who had scrambled around the back of the cliff via the east ledges and were rolling rocks over the rim. The two were discovering that not all climbing hazards are alpine in origin!

"On Yam if you can do a major route then it's a major feather in your cap, if that's what you need."
(Chris Perry)

Brian Spear. Photo Brian Spear collection.

Brian Spear working out the 2nd pitch of *Boomerang* on the first attempt.
Photo Joe Josephson.

Western Union, a climb on the face left of *Unnamed* route at the west end of the cliff, came in the same active year. "I think most of those pitches were unique—it's such a featured wall people can go anywhere up there. I found *Gargoyle* by looking over from *Smeagol*, doing that Yam belay thing where one person's out there working RE-ALLY hard while the other is on belay, drifting—bored or freezing to death. We called it 'cracking the code'—finding the line of a route."

Spear is frank about style, ability, and hero-ism when developing new routes. Discuss-ing the fuss over the bottom-up ethic preva-lent on Yam, the various techniques em-ployed to bolt routes and the use of power drills, he asserts, "How a bolt got in is NOT big news! But, that said, I like travelling light on lead. I like going with a hand drill. I've never placed a hook—I'm into something I call 'stunt drilling' where I'll go to these ri-diculous lengths to get the piece in. I will drill from other gear [hang from a nut or a camming device], though."

He believes the golden age of Yamnuska climbing came ten to twenty years ago, dur-ing what he calls "The Gray Rock Eighties." "Cheesmond was the first to tell us, 'Look, it's an evening crag. You can run up there anytime after work!'" Spear feels most of the activity on the cliff has been "filling in" since then—colouring the spaces between the natural lines.

For the future, Brian believes there are still lines to be climbed—in October of 2001 he put up *Boomerang* with Keith Haberl— and perhaps a variation on present strate-gies could be fruitful. "Maybe there's po-tential for rappel pre-inspection, then ground-up leading? I've been going up there in winter, too, but of course that's old news. And hey, check Nancy Hansen. Her project is to do a different route up there every month for a complete year."

Projects? The future?

"Yam's climbed out."

Spear winks.

Top: Nancy Hanson on *Western Union*.
Bottom: Jeff Moore on attempt 4 (out of 7)
of *Boomerang*. Photos Brian Spear.

The Beat Goes On

In the months between the last interviews for this book in 2002, and the rush to press in the Winter of 2003, significant new activity has occurred on the cliff at Yamnuska. Some of this has been alluded to in the preceding text, but late-breaking news includes the completion of three significant new routes.

In August of 2002, Andy Genereux hooked up with Peter Gatzsch to finish *Cruisin' for a Bruisin'*, a line Andy had been working on solo over the previous year. The route fits between *Dreambed* and *Jimmy and the Cruisers* and crosses *Red Shirt* at that route's crux. Featuring hard 5.11 climbing, the name alludes to a five-metre fall Genereux took when a hook blew during drilling on the 1st pitch.

About the same time, Genereux and Urs Kallen submitted *Glory Days*, a steep and direct linking of cracks immediately left of *Grillmair Chimneys*. Urs had recalled the climb from attempts made in the Seventies by John Lauchlan, Jack Firth and George Homer, and he himself had revisited the line during the years in between with Tim Friesen. Relics and abandoned gear from previous parties extended partway up what is now the 4th pitch of seven all-free pitches featuring climbing up to 5.11c. *Forbidden Fruit*, completed in September of 2002, also by Andy, shadows *Forbidden Corner* closely and finishes up the last pitch of *Milky Way*. As well, a number of shorter climbs have been recently developed on the lower reaches of the eastern end of Yamnuska.

Greg Fletcher on the crux
5th pitch of *Kahl Wall*.
Photo Brian Wyvill.

A Whole New Chapter

A whole new chapter in Yamnuska's history is just beginning with the rediscovery of Big Choss, a collection of modern bouldering problems in the slide area below the main scree slope under the cliff.

The tumbled rocks strewn through the trees there were first explored by the participants and staff of the Rocky Mountain YMCA's Earthways program, who were living in tipis southwest of the quarry during the mid-Seventies. They practiced and option-soloed on the larger formations for a few years before moving on to Canmore and reinventing themselves as a mountaineering school called Yamnuska Inc.

Following that brief period, the big stones stood more or less untouched for 20 years. Recently their rough texture and steep facades have become destinations for the specialized talents and intense scrutiny of the modern bouldering renaissance. Leaders from Calgary like Daren Tremaine, Teresa Abad and Ryan Johnstone began visiting in the fall of '99.

Bouldering-pad-toting traffic to the area has increased steadily since this rediscovery. Easily accessed in any season, Big Choss provides problems of all types and grades up to V9, with many projects awaiting stronger fingers—all this enough to warrant its own place in a guidebook, no doubt appearing soon.

"The attraction slowly grows despite the nearly endless bad rock. It will never be famous, but is one more good reason to live on the eastern slope."
(Daren Tremaine)

Right and above: Shelley Nairn and Chris Fink at Big Choss. Photos Ryan Creary.

4 Hiking the Mountain

Ben Gadd

In this section we present a detailed route description for a complete traverse of Yamnuska, starting up the East Ridge Trail to Raven's End and taking the Eastern Summit Trail to the top, then descending via the Western Summit Trail to Goat Col, continuing along the South Face Trail under Yamnuska's great cliff and finishing down either the East Ridge Trail or the Climber's Trail.

There's a lot of natural history to be enjoyed along the way, so we have included some of that, too.

Warning: travelling the Eastern and Western Summit trails can be hazardous to persons unprepared for rough Canadian Rockies terrain and mountain weather conditions. Further, it's risky to walk under the south face of Yamnuska. Rocks fall from the heights, especially on summer weekends when climbers are busy above. The authors and publishers take no responsibility for anything that may happen to anyone using the information in this guide.

Above: Drawing by Job Kuijt from *Handbook of the Canadian Rockies*.
Opposite: Ben Gadd on the East Ridge Trail. Yamnuska towers above like a crown.

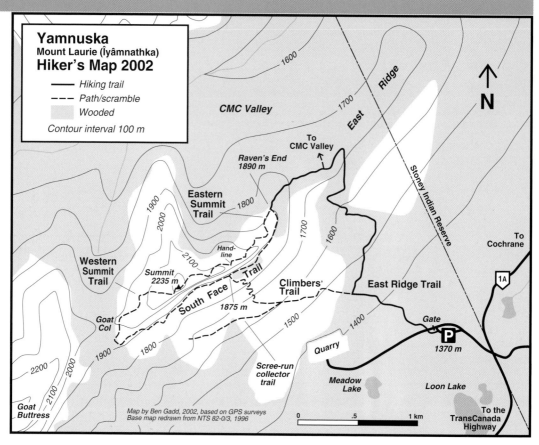

Yamnuska
Mount Laurie (Îyâmnathka)
Hiker's Map 2002
— Hiking trail
--- Path/scramble
▨ Wooded
Contour interval 100 m

CMC Valley

East Ridge

N

To CMC Valley

Raven's End 1890 m

Eastern Summit Trail

Stoney Indian Reserve

To Cochrane

Western Summit Trail

Hand-line

Summit 2235 m

South Face Trail

Climbers' Trail

East Ridge Trail

1875 m

Goat Col

Gate

P 1370 m

Scree-run collector trail

Quarry

Meadow Lake

Loon Lake

Goat Buttress

Map by Ben Gadd, 2002, based on GPS surveys
Base map redrawn from NTS 82-0/3, 1996

0   .5   1 km

To the TransCanada Highway

About the route

Thinking of hiking up the mountain? You're not alone. Many people attempt the climb, and a fair number of them make the summit. But some do not. Getting to the top of Yamnuska is no mere walk; it's a classic Rockies peak-scramble, complete with exposure to height. The elevation gain is 865 m (over 2800 feet), much of it steep. Round-trip times are typically 6-8 hours. Our advice is to get some experience on easier Rockies routes before attempting this one. You may want to bring a climbing harness, two carabiners and some slings, as explained on page 168.

If summitting doesn't sound like your cup of tea, you might still enjoy the first part of the ascent, taking the East Ridge Trail to Raven's End, which is the eastern limit of Yamnuska's huge cliff. This is a fine walk, suitable for anyone who is reasonably fit and has some hiking experience in the Rockies.

It provides rewarding views and offers lots of interesting natural history en route. Give yourself two to three hours to reach the turnaround point at Raven's End and about two-thirds of that to make your way down the same path.

Getting to the Start

To reach Yamnuska from the Trans-Canada Highway between Calgary and Canmore, take the exit for Highway 1X. Go 3.9 km north to Highway 1A. Turn right (east). The road will soon angle left, then straighten. At 2 km from the 1X junction, where 1A angles right, turn off left at a gravel intersection. At the time of writing there was no sign here for Yamnuska access, nor is one planned. From the intersection it's only 300 m to the parking lot. Keep left at the one-way split.

The north side of Yamnuska, showing the summit trails. Photo Alan Kane from *Scrambles in the Canadian Rockies.*

The south face of Yamnuska from the air, showing the South Face Trail and Climber's Trail. Photo Lyn Michaud.

Caution

If you are headed for the summit of the mountain, be aware that the weather can change abruptly at higher elevations, so you'll want to be prepared for rain, wind, sleet and even a summer snowstorm above the treeline. Because the trail is rocky and rubbly in its higher reaches, you may wish to wear over-the-ankle shoes. Light hiking boots are ideal.

Carry plenty of water. There is no reliable supply along the way, and Yamnuska's slopes are often dry and sunny, hot on a summer afternoon. You may find yourself drinking a litre of liquid per hour.

Trail Log
Distances in Kilometres

Aspen forest along the East Ridge Trail.
Photo Chic Scott.

Leafy trees
If it's a leafy tree, you have only three choices: **aspen** (*Populus tremuloides*, with smooth bark and fairly small, rounded leaves), **balsam poplar** (*Populus balsamifera*, also called cottonwood, with smooth bark on young trees and rough-ribbed gray bark on older trees, both with larger, more pointed leaves than those of aspen) or **white birch** (*Betula papyrifera*, short trees at low elevations, with pale bark that is peeling from the trunk, showing orange beneath, and rather small, ragged-edged leaves).

East Ridge Trail

0.0 Trailhead at the west end of the Yamnuska parking lot, elevation 1370 m. This is the beginning for both the East Ridge Trail and the Climber's Trail. The wide path crosses the quarry access road shortly—no public traffic here, beyond the gate—and begins its climb through aspen groves.

Flowering plants to watch for along the opening stretch of the trail include wild rose, buffaloberry, snowberry, cow parsnip, honeysuckle, clematis, wild sweet pea, harebell, sweetvetch, wild strawberry, northern bedstraw, yarrow, arnica, geranium, meadow rue, paintbrush, Solomon's seal and false Solomon's seal. Western wood lily is the showiest thing on the mountain; watch for its big orange flowers in late June and early July. Later in the summer look for the pink of fireweed and the yellow of ragwort, goldenrod and wild gaillardia.

This kind of broad-leaf forest is the right habitat for flycatchers, vireos, white-throated sparrows and thrushes; for white-tailed deer, mule deer and elk, for snowshoe hares and coyotes. Bears? Yes, but seldom seen along such a popular route.

0.5 Cross a dirt track. (Not far up this old road, co-author Chic Scott pitched his tent and lived in it for three months in 1997, saving money while he wrote some of his classic Canadian climbing history *Pushing the Limits.*) The trail then climbs steeply through low thickets of saskatoon and dogbane along a slope rubbly with chunks of reddish Chungo sandstone, a hard layer that is quarried for silicon in the nearby pit operated by Lafarge Canada. Rocky Mountain maple also grows along this section of the trail.

0.8 Main junction atop the first bench, elevation 1470 m. The Climber's Trail continues straight ahead; the East Ridge Trail goes right. A path to the left goes a short distance to the Practice Cliff, which is a house-high outcrop of Chungo sandstone popular for teaching rock climbing basics. Turn right and continue on the East Ridge Trail. It follows the level bench. Listen for the robin-like songs of vireos and the reedy calls of flycatchers.

1.2 Minor junction with the old beginning of the East Ridge Trail, which comes in from the left. Called in those days the "Horse Trail," it originally started at the sandstone quarry. Keep right.

1.4 Cross a dry drainage and enter a mixed-wood forest of lodgepole pine, white spruce, Douglas-fir and aspen, with a few small white-birch trees. The trail soon crosses a somewhat larger drainage, typically dry but with an intermittent spring farther up, then it swings left to climb steeply along the side of this drainage. The slope is dry and fairly open between the aspens, with kinnikinnik and juniper as groundcover. You may see the small yellow flowers of stonecrop, a drought-resistant member of the sedum family.

   The trail breaks up here, with paths a few metres apart that cross and re-cross. To avoid further erosion along the steeper lines, take the gentler choices. Everything joins again 200 m higher. The trail leaves the gully and angles right, climbing across a grassy hillside with small stands of wind-stunted aspens. Lots of kinnikinnik covers the ground here, and you'll see two kinds of juniper bushes: creeping juniper (cedar-like branches with smooth needles, very low-growing, spreading over the ground) and common juniper (very prickly, up to knee-high).

2.1 Trail steepens and splits briefly. The upper segment is in the trees—shady on a hot day—while the lower one is in the open and gives better views.

2.5 Trail splits again. Most hikers follow the left branch, but you may want to keep right here and walk a short distance to a lovely spot for a rest. Outcrops of Belly

Lodgepole pine *(Pinus contorta)*
These trees are easy to identify by their needles, which are longer than those of the other species. They grow in pairs. The cones are woody and hard.

White spruce *(Picea glauca)*
Of the two kinds of spruces on Yamnuska, these grow at low elevations along the trail. Check the needles. They are short and rather sharp. Diamond-shaped in cross-section, a spruce needle will roll between your thumb and your finger. The cones are papery. Check the individual scales on the cones. If the edges of the scales are round and smooth, like the edge of a well-manicured fingernail, you're looking at a white spruce. If the edges are rough, it might be …

Douglas-fir *(Pseudotsuga menziesii)*
Note the hyphen in the name, indicating that this tree is not a true fir; that is, it's not of the genus *Abies*. To differentiate Douglas-fir from subalpine fir, check the cones. The cones of true firs stand upright on the branch and shed their scales one at a time, until only the central cone-stalks are left. Douglas-fir cones hang down from the branches, and the scales don't fall off. Stuck onto each scale is a strap-like bract (see illustration) that looks rather like the short tail and hind legs of a tiny mouse hiding its head in the cone—as an old Blackfoot story about this tree goes.

Drawings by Job Kuijt from
Handbook of the Canadian Rockies.

The view over the Bow Valley from the East Ridge Trail. Photo Chic Scott.

Yamnuska from the East Ridge Trail. Photo Chic Scott.

River sandstone offer natural seating for an outstanding panorama. Spread out before you is the Bow Valley—particularly lovely in autumn, when the many aspen groves are golden—with the river winding across the grasslands of Morley Flats. Across the flats lie the wooded Rocky Mountain foothills. The cliffy gray limestone peaks and ridges of the mountain front stretch away to the south. Closer at hand Yamnuska looms above, looking like a castle or a royal crown.

From these outcrops a rough path continues east, eventually cresting the ridge and heading back toward Yamnuska, where it rejoins the East Ridge Trail. But there are several variants along the way, and it's easy to wind up on one of the paths down the northern side of the ridge by mistake. So we recommend that you return to the East Ridge Trail proper.

Back at the junction, the East Ridge Trail angles fairly steeply toward the top of the ridge. Then it turns left and levels off, following the side of the ridge atop meadowy slopes that present good views to the south. After 200 m it turns right and climbs very steeply to the broad ridge crest.

2.9 Main junction atop the ridge, elevation 1740 m. Take the branch heading west (left) toward the mountain; turning north (right) takes you over the ridge and down the other side to CMC Valley (the name comes from Calgary Mountain Club; see page 39).

Continuing westward toward Yamnuska along the open left side of the ridge crest, you reach another split 150 m farther on, a minor one in which the two trails parallel each other a few metres apart. Keep right; the lower path is used in winter and early spring to avoid deep snow along the upper path. They rejoin after 100 m, where the main trail enters the woods. Stay on the more heavily used path at any other splits along the ridge.

The trees in this section are mostly spruces that are intermediate between pure white spruce and pure Engelmann spruce.

These two species are distinct at low elevations (white spruce only) and near the treeline (Engelmann spruce only), but between these extremes the trees show characteristics of both.

And have you noticed the boulders and chunks of gray limestone along this section of the route? Up to now, there has been little limestone; the bedrock here is Belly River sandstone. The limestone material was dragged eastward along the ridge by glaciers at least 15,000 years ago and perhaps 65,000 years ago. Thus, the gray pieces can be termed *erratics:* glacially transported rocks. The source of the erratics is the east end of Yamnuska's enormous cliff, as seen ahead through the trees.

Once it has gained the ridge, the trail climbs fairly steeply, sometimes emerging from the trees for views of CMC Valley to the north (right) and the cliffs that border it: left to right, Wakonda Buttress, Bilbo Buttress and Frodo Buttress. The latter two names come from J.R.R. Tolkien's *The Lord of the Rings*, which was very popular reading in the 1970s when Calgary Mountain Club climbers were making first ascents in the area. "Wakonda" is attributed to CMC member George Homer, originally from Liverpool, who used the Liverpudlian "wak"—slang for "my friend"—to describe his climbing partner Billy Davidson as "wak-on-da-wall" ("my friend on the wall") while the two of them made the first ascent of the overhanging face in 1971.

3.5 The east end of Yamnuska's great cliff, elevation 1890 m. This spot is increasingly being called "Raven's End," after the locale in Ben Gadd's popular novel of that title, published in 2001. Yes, ravens do frequent the place. So do pikas, the small rodent-like lagomorphs that play a part in the story.

For many hikers, this is a good destination for the day's walk. From here to the summit, the route is no longer a hike. It's a scramble, meaning that in places you'll be using your hands as well as your feet.

Engelmann spruce *(Picea engelmannii)*
Look for these at higher elevations, near and at the treeline. The needles are similar to those of white spruce, although a bit more upwardly curved, but the real difference is in the cones: the edges of the scales are not smooth and round. They are ragged-looking and shaped the way a screwdriver blade is ground (see illustration). Specimens at treeline will show this best; lower down you will find spruces that have cone scales with less ragged, more rounded edges— but not as smooth-edged and round-edged as those of white spruce. These intermediates between white spruce and Engelmann spruce are referred to by foresters as "white x Engelmann," meaning "white crossed with Engelmann."

Drawing by Job Kuijt from *Handbook of the Canadian Rockies.*

Pika *(Ochotona princeps)*
Drawing by Matthew Wheeler from *Handbook of the Canadian Rockies.*

Raven *(Corvus corax)*
Drawing by Matthew Wheeler from
Handbook of the Canadian Rockies.

Golden-mantled ground squirrel
(Spermophilus lateralis)
Photo Gillean Daffern.

Thus, Raven's End is a popular turnaround point. It's a good spot for lunch—which is one reason that ravens check the place out frequently, hoping for messy eaters. While enjoying your sandwiches, expect a visit from a golden-mantled ground squirrel. These friendly rodents are striped on their backs rather like chipmunks, but chipmunk species also have stripes on their faces, while the golden-mantled ground squirrel has a white ring around each eye.

When you step onto the gray limestone here, you have crossed a fault: the McConnell Thrust, which underlies the cliff-ringed summit block of the mountain and separates it from the gentler terrain to the east. This fault is a major one. It runs along the base of the mountain front from just south of the Bow River nearly to the Athabasca River, a distance of over 300 km, and it divides the front ranges of the Rockies on the western side of the fault from the foothills on the eastern side. The exact trace of the fault is hidden under rock debris at Raven's End, but it can be seen up close along the western section of the South Face Trail (see pages 174 and 175).

This kind of faulting places older rock atop younger rock. At Yamnuska the McConnell Thrust has pushed a thick sheet of middle Cambrian limestone (the Eldon Formation, about 525 million years old), up and over sandstone and shale of the Belly River Formation, about 80 million years old. Further, the Eldon limestone sheet has been shoved 15–45 km northeastward, sliding along on the younger layers beneath. When you step over that fault you're crossing 445 million years of geological time and taking a magical leap in distance.

As an alternative descent from Raven's End, you can hike the gentle eastern half of the South Face Trail and then head down the steep Climber's Trail. Although this route back down the mountain is not a scramble, do be aware that the Climber's Trail can be tough on the knees. The South Face Trail begins at Raven's End, heading off to the southwest (left as you face the rocks). Following this for 0.7 km will bring you to a junction with the Climber's Trail, which you can then descend for 2.1 km to the base of the mountain. (For a description of what you see along the South Face Trail and the Climber's Trail, see pages 173-177.)

Eastern Summit Trail

To continue, scramble through the obvious cleft in the limestone—don't bother going around to the right; it looks easier that way but isn't—and emerge onto Yamnuska's northeastern slope. You're now on the Eastern Summit Trail, a rough path that almost immediately loses its definition for a short distance. Make your way up over scree-covered rock until the route becomes better defined, consisting of several parallel paths angling fairly steeply across the bowl below the ridge. (Trails seen cutting across the bowl lower down are bighorn sheep paths. They don't go to the summit.)

3.9 By the time you reach the far side of the bowl, the paths have converged. Scramble 15 m up to a gap in a rock spur. The Eastern Summit Trail continues easily beyond, soon coming close to the ridge crest. From here you can scramble up to a smashing view out over the south face to the Bow Valley. Or look straight down the section of cliff called the Bowl (careful!) to the sloping meadows far below.

At this point your elevation is roughly 2000 m and you are close to the treeline, meaning the upper elevational limit of tree growth. Short, gnarled Engelmann spruces—pure Engelmann, not crosses with white spruce—and subalpine firs lead tough lives up here, surviving winds that exceed 100 km/h, abrasive blowing snow, temperatures as low as -40°C and very dry air. The growing season is quite short, typically from late June until the end of August. At treeline there just aren't enough days in the summer with temperatures warm enough to allow a tree to grow new twigs and needles in time for the twigs to "harden off"—that is, to become wood—before winter comes.

At Raven's End. The Eastern Summit Trail starts here and passes through the narrow cleft at upper left. Photo Chic Scott.

Subalpine fir *(Abies lasiocarpa)* Again, check the needles. If they are flat—won't roll between your thumb and your finger—then you have either a subalpine fir, which is a true fir, or a Douglas-fir, which isn't. Near the treeline, flat-needled conifers on Yamnuska are always subalpine firs. But along the South Face Trail or lower on the mountain they might be Douglas-firs as described on page 161.

Drawing by Job Kuijt from *Handbook of the Canadian Rockies.*

Ascending the Eastern Summit Trail.
Photo Chic Scott.

Townsend's solitaire *(Myadestes townsendi)*
Drawing by Matthew Wheeler from
Handbook of the Canadian Rockies.

Purple Saxifrage *(Saxifraga oppositifolia)*
Drawing by Job Kuijt from
Handbook of the Canadian Rockies.

If you arrive here early in the season, while there are still snow patches on the ground, you may see small, delicate flowers of purple saxifrage blooming on cushions of tiny leaves that look like miniature hen-and-chickens plants. Another cushion plant growing at these elevations is alpine potentilla, with buttercup-like flowers. It's actually in the rose family, as is white dryas, a ground-covering shrub you'll see here. (See page 173 for drawing). The small, scallop-edged leaves lie close to the ground, and the decorative star-shaped white flowers don't rise much above it. In late summer the seedheads look like those of dandelions. These are all truly alpine species, preferring rocky, cool, windy locations such as this one. (White dryas has a similar-leaved, yellow-blooming relative that grows much lower down.)

Two knee-high shrubs growing along the trail are easy to identify: rock willow has deeply veined, leathery leaves, and dwarf birch has small green leaves with toothy edges.

At treeline on Yamnuska you may hear the long, twittery, wren-like song of the Townsend's solitaire. It's a rather ordinary-looking robin-size bird—like the robin a member of the thrush family—that is mostly gray with a white eye ring and rather long, dark tailfeathers with a white feather on each side. Townsend's solitaire sits by itself atop a conifer and sings and sings. This is a bird worth listening for, a classic Rockies species that figures in the *Raven's End* story.

Bighorn sheep *(Ovis canadensis)*.
Photo Gillean Daffern.

From here the summit looks close and the way on seems straightforward. But that's a false impression. The true summit is out of sight higher up, and the route becomes more difficult. The trail becomes harder to follow, and you have to cross some rocky ledges.

4.3 The summit you see in the distance is now the true summit. Here the trail crosses steeper slopes on more rocky ledges. Take your time and place your feet carefully.

Soon you approach the edge of the south face. The trail doesn't quite reach the cliff, but if you step up a few metres to it you can see where the climbing route *Grillmair Chimneys* (climbed in 1952) finishes at the left end of a flat spot, and uniquely: through a hole just back from the edge!

You are now in the sort of terrain preferred by bighorn sheep. You may see their tracks, their droppings, perhaps the animals themselves, few and wary on Yamnuska after many years of local hunting pressure. If you see a hoofed animal that is all white, not brown or gray with a white rear end and a dark tail, then you have seen a mountain goat. Consider yourself lucky.

On the Very Scary Traverse. Photo Chic Scott.

4.5 Just around the next corner and marked by a cairn (stack of rocks), is the Very Scary Traverse, a line of ledges leading horizontally across a cliff—not Yamnuska's great south face, but a cliff nonetheless—for 20 m. This obstacle has turned around many a hiker in the past, but in 2002 a sturdy steel-cable handline was installed along the traverse to make it safer. As with any wilderness hiker's aid—a trail, a bridge, whatever—you use the handline at your own risk. It's like the "via ferratas" of the Euro-

On the Very Scary Traverse. Photo Chic Scott.

pean Alps, in which much longer lengths of cable are anchored to the rocks for anyone to use. You may wish to bring a climbing harness and cross this section via-ferrata style, attached to the cable with two carabiners that connect short slings to the harness. The carabiners slide along the cable. You unclip one sling when you reach a cable-attachment point, clip it on again past the point, then move the second sling past the point, and so on.

An alternative to the Very Scary Traverse is to climb up to the crest of the ridge and bypass the cliff. But if go that way you'll have to down-climb steeply-sloping rock along the ridge, with the true south face right beside you and no handline to hold onto—an even scarier proposition. Thus, a third alternative is sometimes chosen here: go back the way you came. There's no shame in that; your mother wouldn't like to see you up there on the Very Scary Traverse anyway.

Looking back toward the Very Scary Traverse (far peak) and the complex terrain that follows it. Photo Chic Scott.

The view from the top looking back down the Eastern Summit Trail. Photo Chic Scott.

Beyond the traverse you pass by a cleft that drops away down the south face. This is the top of the classic route *Chockstone Corner* (first ascent 1963).

Continue along ledges for 40 m to another cliff edge, and avoid a second traverse by scrambling up a few metres along the edge and crossing it easily. The path passes by another cleft in the south face—the top of the *Bottleneck* route (1964)—and then descends sharply for 30 m in a wide, rocky gully. Go left around the corner into a second gully, this one full of soft scree that you slog up for 30 m or so, then you head over to the right to reach a ridge. On the other side the last slope leads easily to the summit.

5.0 Summit of Yamnuska, elevation 2235 m. You have gained 865 m to reach it. The Western Summit Trail to the top is plainly visible on the slope below.

Yam's highest point is a rocky, windy, lightning-prone place that shouldn't occupy more of your time than it has to. Consider the weather and head down right away if it looks like a storm might be on its way.

Still, it is surprising what can grow in such hostile locations. Mushrooms, for example, sometimes pop up in a bed of white dryas within a few metres of the summit cairn.

Ben Gadd at the summit. Photo Chic Scott.

Where are all the jets going?
Unless the sky is cloudy, you're bound to see several passenger jets flying over Yamnuska while you're hiking on the mountain. That's because Yamnuska lies right below the usual flight path from Calgary to Vancouver.

In 2001 climber Jason McLeod was in a car crash that nearly took his life: he was hit head-on by a drunk driver. As a goal to regaining his health, he challenged himself to ascend Yamnuska. On March 28, 2002, a year to the day after the accident, he climbed the mountain in the company of Rob Torkildson, Laurie Skreslet, Pat Morrow, Jerry Kobalenko and other close friends. In the photo he is approaching the summit from the Western Summit Trail. Photo Ben Smailes.

Western Summit Trail

5.3 After starting down the Western Summit Trail, you'll find that it splits. The main route is the right branch, heading down a steep patch of scree that is fun to descend quickly by taking big steps or even leaping. The left branch takes you over into the rocks and is not recommended. Don't go too far down the scree; you may miss the proper continuation and wind up in CMC Valley. This might be a good idea, though. It's a fantastic scree run, and connecting paths allow you to walk eastward around the north side of Yamnuska and back up to the East Ridge Trail, thus completing a circumnavigation of the mountain. (This fine outing will be detailed in the fourth edition of Gillean Daffern's *Kananaskis Country Trail Guide*, Volume 1.)

However, back to the present route. The Western Summit Trail angles off to the left some 60 m down the scree run, goes around the corner of the mountain and crosses a rocky, slabby section—poor footing—where it is washed out and faint. The path can be seen beyond the rocks, however, leading down to ...

5.7 Goat Col, the treeline saddle between Yamnuska and Goat Mountain, which is the big rock buttress to the west. There is a fin-like outcrop of limestone here, about 2 m high. It has provided shelter from the wind for many people on this trail, even serving as an overnight bivouac spot on occasion. What those shelterers may not have known is that the overhanging side is the upper surface of a small thrust fault that divides the Eldon limestone of the fin from the orange-weathering rubble of the Pika Formation on the slope above. The Pika is the next rock unit above the Eldon. It is also a middle Cambrian limestone, but more easily eroded than the Eldon, so that only a patch of it remains on the mountain, extending from here up to the rocky, slabby area you just crossed. This fault runs right across Goat Col, from southeast to northwest.

Looking back at the summit from the Western Summit Trail. Photo Chic Scott.

Goat Col. View of the Western Summit Trail angling up to the left. Path at centre is a climber's track. The fin-like outcrop (circled) sticks up just above the figure. Photo Gillean Daffern.

Setting off along the South Face Trail from the west end of Yamnuska.
The maximum cliff height is 360 m. Photo Chic Scott.

Past the rock fin, the barren slope is adorned with patches of white dryas and scattered small cushions of alpine potentilla. The yellow flowers are buttercup-like and showy as they wave about in the breeze. Shrubby cinquefoil, their larger relative, also grows here and may be in bloom; the flowers are similar.

Any paths seen branching to the right in Goat Col lead northward into CMC Valley. Keep left.

The slope down from the col is steep, and the surface, while not bedrock, is hard. It's littered with loose rock fragments, so tread carefully or risk a skidding fall.

South Face Trail

The trail curves left and then levels out as it starts to follow the base of Yamnuska's huge cliff eastward, along the top of a steep slope. This is now the South Face Trail. The footing is bouldery and sometimes unstable through this section; watch your step. All that rubble came from the cliff above, so listen for the cracking, whizzing sound of rockfall. Pay special attention on weekends when climbers are often up there.

Some of the classic climbing routes on this face are plainly visible. We have pointed them out in the description of the South Face Trail that follows.

6.4 Just after passing a grove of trees, look back westward to an obvious slot in the cliff. There is a tooth-like tower at the top. Just below, a big orange pumpkin has been painted on the rock (see page 60 for the reason). This is *Unnamed* route (1961). To the left is the shorter slot of *King's Chimney* (1964). More directly above, the huge corner with the big overhang and another tooth at the top is *Belfry* (1957).

A hundred metres farther you reach a big scree bowl that offers a quick, very steep descent from the trail you are on. Several tracks head straight down to a collector trail at the base of the scree bowl. This collector ties in with the Climber's Trail. The scars of

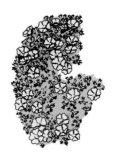

Alpine potentilla
(Potentilla nivea)

Shrubby potentilla
(Potentilla fruticosa)

White dryas
(Dryas octopetala)

Drawings by Job Kuijt from
Handbook of the Canadian Rockies.

the various scree runs are wide and obvious, visible even from the Trans-Canada Highway many kilometres away.

6.7 At this point you're right below the summit. *Direttissima* (1957) goes straight up that wide gray groove above you, while *Calgary Route* (1953, second oldest climb on Yamnuska) takes the obvious cleft to the left. Between the two is the buff-coloured, overhanging line of *CMC Wall* (1972). To the right of *Direttissima* is the blank-looking Suicide Wall, ascended via the newer routes *Astro Yam* (1986) on its left side and *Above and Beyond* (also 1986) to the right. These sections of the cliff illustrate a rule about rock colour that Yamnuska climbers quickly come to know: gray rock is vertical or less steep, while yellowish rock is overhanging.

Looking up *Grillmair Chimneys*.
Photo Glenn Reisenhofer.

6.9 Where the trail runs beside a short rock wall set below the main face, look up toward a large overhanging crack, the line taken by *Balrog* (1969). It was the most difficult and frightening of the early routes, perhaps Brian Greenwood's greatest achievement on Yamnuska. *Balrog* still has a fierce reputation, but at time of writing a younger generation of climbers is putting up an even harder route just to its right, one that punches directly through the overhangs.

7.0 The trail curves around the top of a steep slope of dark Belly River shale. This bowl-like feature is the most difficult obstacle along the South Face Trail. The path, even though it is heavily used—or perhaps *because* it is heavily used—is little more than a dent in the slope in places, and the footing is poor. Be very careful, for a slip here could lead to a painful slide.

Before you start this section, though, take a moment to look up. The prominent gash in the face ahead of you is the route of *Grillmair Chimneys* (1952), the first rock-climber's line on Yamnuska. The last pitch is in the spectacular, vertical chimney at the top. Directly above you are the crack systems of *Chockstone Corner* (1963) and *Bottleneck* (1964), finishing at points you passed along the upper Eastern Summit Trail. These two climbing routes cross partway up the face, such that *Chockstone Corner* begins left of *Bottleneck* but finishes in the right-hand crack, while *Bottleneck* finishes in the left-hand crack.

7.1 As you near the east side of the shale bowl, where the path is at its narrowest and most treacherous, you walk right beside the McConnell Thrust. This horizontal fault divides dark, coal-bearing Cretaceous shale beds of the Belly River Formation from the buff-coloured Cambrian limestone of the Eldon Formation above. Generations of geologists have hiked up Yamnuska to see the McConnell Thrust here, because elsewhere the fault trace is covered by rubble or vegetation.

Whitish crusts on the shale along the fault are deposits of calcium chloride left from groundwater moving along the fault and evaporating in the dry air here. Note how thin the fault zone is. You can stick a knife blade into it. The rock above and below the break shows signs of disturbance, but not nearly as much as that seen along major faults that are not thrust faults. Non-thrusted faults are typically marked by a zone of crushed rock. Here the limestone rests on the shale as if it were simply another bed in the sequence of layers. Yet the limestone block above the fault has slid 15–45 km northeastward (to the right) along the slippery coal beds below.

7.2 Main junction, elevation 1875 m. Downhill to the right is the Climber's Trail, so named because it provides quick access to routes up the south face. Straight ahead is the continuation of the South Face Trail, which becomes much easier to follow than it has been. There are more climbing routes to see in that direction, so why not go that way, reconnect with the East Ridge Trail and follow it back down to the parking lot, the way you came up? The Climber's Trail is shorter, but much steeper. (We have still described it for you, beginning on page 177, if you really want to go down that way.)

Following the eastern branch of the South Face Trail, you stay quite close to the base of the cliff for a while. The imposingly vertical rock above does have a classic route on it: the difficult *Kahl Wall* (1971).

The trail branches. Look up at this point and a little back. You'll see a large inside corner that runs a long way up the face. This is *Forbidden Corner* (1964), another well-loved route.

Ben pointing out the McConnell Thrust, the major fault that underlies Yamnuska. Rock above the pole has slid along the fault a distance of 15-45 km from left to right. Photo Chic Scott.

Drawings by Matthew Wheeler from
Handbook of the Canadian Rockies.

Red-tailed hawk *(Buteo jumaicensis)*

Prairie Falcon *(Falco mexicanus)*

Gollum Grooves. Photo from CMC log book.

Take the right branch of the trail, into the trees. The path moves away from the face a little. Where it crosses an outcrop of gray limestone, look back over your shoulder and find the crack-and-corner system of *Red Shirt* (1962), the most popular line on this part of the cliff. Directly above you is the Bowl, a very steep, dished part of the face that was first climbed a little right of centre along a route of the same name (1965). The right edge of the Bowl, on the skyline ahead of you, is the Yellow Edge.

You may hear the hungry cries of young ravens above you in the Bowl, a favourite place for these birds to nest. Red-tailed hawks may be seen here, too, and sometimes a prairie falcon.

7.5 You're directly below the Yellow Edge, a name applied to both the physical feature and the difficult climbing route forced up it in 1974. The *Yellow Edge* route follows the right side of the sharp arête, through the overhangs. Another famous route also begins here: *Corkscrew* (1967). As its name implies, *Corkscrew* is a complex line. It scales the cliff in a series of vertical sections linked by short traverses. *Corkscrew* starts close to the Yellow Edge and trends generally right.

7.7 After a section of trail that is more open, you reach the trees again. Look for an obvious deep crack high on the face. That's the final pitch of *Pangolin* (1965), named, oddly enough, for a type of anteater. East of *Pangolin* the south face becomes more broken, with extensive crack systems that have become the popular routes *Smeagol* (1970), *Dick's Route* (1970) and *Gollum Grooves* (1962). By this time the early Yam climbers must have been running out of names, because the last three routes they established before reaching the end of the cliff are simply named *A Route*, *B Route* and *C Route*, all climbed in the mid-1960s.

7.9 You're now back at Raven's End, where you can take the East Ridge Trail the rest of the way down the mountain.

Descending the Climber's Trail

0.0 Junction with the South Face Trail, elevation 1875 m. A steep, switchbacking descent begins. The slope is mostly open, with small subalpine firs and Engelmann spruces growing on it, and a few lodgepole pines. Kinnikinnik (pronounce it any way you like; it's also called "bearberry") is the main groundcover. It's a low-growing shrub with evergreen leaves. In May it blooms: little white urn-like flowers, pink at the opening, nectar-laden and thus eagerly sought by queen bumblebees that have survived the winter pregnant, ready to start a new swarm. In September and later, watch for the bright red berries of this plant, mealy and loaded with starch. Aboriginal peoples across Canada have pounded up kinnikinnik berries with any sort of fat to produce the trail-food "pemmican."

The southern slope of Yamnuska offers habitat for meadow-loving wildflowers such as harebell, yarrow, ragwort, goldenrod, wild gaillardia and western wood lily.

0.8 Entering from the right is the collector trail from the scree-run descent paths.

1.2 An old, overly steep trail comes in from the left. Once used as a quick descent route from Raven's End, this path is now badly eroded. It needs time to revegetate.

1.5 Cross the old trail from the quarry.

1.6 Junction with the East Ridge Trail. Straight ahead to the parking lot, less than a kilometre away.

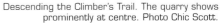

Descending the Climber's Trail. The quarry shows prominently at centre. Photo Chic Scott.

Glossary

Rock climbing has developed its own idiomatic version of English. Here are some rough translations of terms, just in case you've lent this book to your mother or something.

aid (noun) Various methods of using climbing hardware to assist progress over difficult passages of rock. The opposite of "free."

artificial climbing (noun) Same as "aid."

bolt (noun, verb) An industrial-spec masonry anchor, placed in a shallow hole drilled by hand with a bit and hammer or with the aid of a cordless rotary hammer. The act of installing such hardware on a climb.

cam, Friend, SLCD (nouns) An active camming device. Typically larger, but can be used more places and with greater security than nuts.

choss (noun) Dirty, friable, unappealing or otherwise poor-quality rock.

dyno (noun, verb) Any dynamic movement by a climber on the rock, where one hold is released in order to lunge toward another.

ex-WD (adjective) Ex-War Department, the British equivalent of "army surplus."

FA (noun) First ascent.

fatty (noun) Marijuana cigarette.

FFA (noun) First free ascent.

free (verb, adjective, adverb) attempting to climb using the rock only, without hanging or pulling on any ropes or hardware. Modifying "route," "attempt,"etc.

grit ethic (noun) Climbing as if on the gritstone outcrops of England, where the leader is expected to use only "natural protection," placed while he or she climbs. The consequences of failure can be severe.

hook (noun, verb) Piece of shaped steel with bent and sharpened tip, the length of a finger. The act of using same to hang from small edges of rock.

jug (noun, verb) A large handhold. To ascend a rope using Jumar-brand clamps, whose handles are like those on beer pitchers.

laid rope (adjective) Manufactured with twists like a boat rope, rather than braided like today's climbing ropes.

mank, manky (noun, adjective) Same as "choss," but with connotations of damp and/or rot.

nut (noun) Small piece of metal (looks like a machine nut) on a wire cable that can be lodged in a crack without hammering to arrange convenient protection.

opening (verb) Presenting a modern route in a state ready to be climbed free, with permanent hardware installed, belay stances defined and loose rock cleared away, though not necessarily having climbed it cleanly oneself.

option-solo (verb) To go alone over easy terrain, opting to attempt harder passages whenever the feeling is right.

pin, peg (nouns, verbs) Same as "piton."

piton (noun, verb) A short metal spike with an eye or ring for attaching a carabiner. Hammered into a crack in the rock to secure a rope. Describes the act of placement.

protection (noun) Running anchors for the rope between the climber and the belayer.

pumpy (adjective) Causing the forearms to become engorged with blood from effort, whereupon they ache and lose strength.

redpoint (verb) Finally climb a pitch "free" after a number of failed attempts.

run-out (noun) The distance between pieces of protection on a climb. The longer this is, the longer and potentially more injurious a fall will be. From the act of 'running out' the rope while climbing on lead.

send (verb) Climb successfully in the style desired, usually "free," with no falls.

simul-climb (verb) Party moving together for speed or convenience while connected by the rope which passes through protection.

slab (noun) Compact, less-than-vertical rock, requiring friction technique to climb.

sport climb (noun) A convenient climb with all anchors permanently installed, where a fall from anywhere on the route would be relatively safe and without risk of injury.

tri-cam (noun) An unusually shaped slung nut that can be set in awkward positions.

wire, chock (nouns) same as "nut."

Index

The Authors

Chic Scott, a fourth-generation Albertan, was in the first wave of Canadians who worked their way into the sport dominated at the time by British and European immigrants. During the 1960s Chic learned to climb on Yamnuska, then went on to travel the globe, climbing in Europe and the Himalaya. He is perhaps best known for his high-level ski traverses in the Rockies and Columbia Mountains.

Chic is an energetic organiser and has served on numerous committees for both the Calgary Mountain Club and the Alpine Club of Canada. In 1978 he founded the Canadian Himalayan Foundation and in 1996 the John Lauchlan Award. For his contributions to leadership and his commitment to documenting Canada's climbing history, he was awarded the 2000 Summit of Excellence Award at the Banff Mountain Film Festival.

Chic presently earns his living as a writer and lecturer. He has written four books including the award-winning *Pushing the Limits; The Story of Canadian Mountaineering*. In 2002 Chic had to pay income tax for the first time in 15 years. "Now that's real success!"

Dave Dornian first climbed on Yamnuska when he was 16. He and his partner took turns exchanging a hockey helmet and a motorcycle helmet, and relied on unsecured sitting hip belays while they struggled up *Unnamed*. Since then, Dornian has climbed for more than 30 years on Yamnuska, in Canada and abroad.

He is presently the chair of the Alpine Club of Canada's Competition Climbing Committee and director of the North American Council for Competition Climbing, as well as the negligent editor of the notorious *Calgary Mountain Club World News*.

Dave has a post-graduate degree in philosophy and works as a journalist and writer, reviewing films and books that feature the outdoor recreation community. He is a regular contributor to climbing and outdoor magazines in Canada and the US, and has also contributed to a number of books about climbing in the Rocky Mountains.

Ben Gadd has lived in or near the Rockies all his life. Educated as a geologist, he has pursued a career in natural history and become a recognized authority on the Rocky Mountains. In addition to writing and teaching about this great mountain region, he designs nature trails, produces interpretive signage and advises protected-area managers.

Fresh up from Colorado, Ben did his first route on Yamnuska in 1969: *Grillmair Chimneys*. "I was terrified," he recalls. "These Canadian Rockies cliffs were huge, with an oversupply of portable handholds." But he went on to enjoy many a climb on Yam's south face.

Ben is the author of *Handbook of the Canadian Rockies* and six other books. His first novel, *Raven's End*, is a best-seller—much of the story taking place on and around Yamnuska.

Left to right: Ben Gadd, Chic Scott and Dave Dornian below the east end of Yamnuska. Photo Gillean Daffern.

Flying a kite on the summit of Yamnuska. Photo Chic Scott.

Acknowledgements

Chic Scott would like to thank Urs Kallen for suggesting we celebrate the fiftieth anniversary of climbing on Yamnuska with a book.

Thank you to those who shared their homes and their stories with me: Hans Gmoser, Leo Grillmair, Dick Howe, Klaus Hahn, Franz Dopf, Ken Pawson, Don Vockeroth, Isabel Spreat, Hans and Lilo Fuhrer, John Martin, Urs Kallen, Chris Perry and Tim Auger.

Thank you to those who contributed photographs and other material: John Martin, Leo Grillmair, Ferdl Taxbock, Hans Fuhrer, Gunti Prinz, Hans Gmoser, Jim Tarrant, Marj Hind, Ron Robinson, Isabel Spreat, Don Vockeroth, Inge Stolz, Klaus Hahn, Glen Boles, Jon Jones, Tim Auger, Perry Davis, Rob Owens, Chris Perry, Maja Swannie, Jeff Horne, Ron Langevin, Urs Kallen, Trevor Jones, Bill Browne, Dave Campbell, Dave Morgan and Ben Smailes.

Thank you to those who contributed images to past projects which have been used again in this book: Philippe Delesalle, Franz Dopf, Ron Thomson, Diana Knaak, Dick Lofthouse, Neil Bennett, Steve DeMaio, Kevin Doyle, Barry Blanchard, Jeff Marshall, Alan Derbyshire and Ben Firth.

Dave Dornian would like to thank for their contributions to the story of the modern era of climbing on Yamnuska: Tim Auger, Barry Blanchard, Dave Campbell, Keith Carter, Steve DeMaio, Allan Derbyshire, Kevin Doyle, Marc Dube, Jeff Everett, Ben Firth, Greg Fletcher, Todd Guyn, Keith Haberl, Jon Jones, Trevor Jones, Ryan Johnstone, William Marler, Pat Morrow, Sharon Parker, Chris Perry, Choc Quinn, Glenn Reisenhofer, Raphael Slawinski, Brian Spear, Shep Steiner, Maja Swannie, Brian Wyvill and Colin Zacharias for interviews, follow-ups, photos, and uncut gems dropped into casual conversation. Bless Chic (who had the idea for the book in the first place, and kept pressing me with references and tips). Praise Joe Josephson, Jeff Marshall, Tim Mooney and Bill Stark for not only telling their stories, but for reviewing and ever-so-gently correcting howlers in the first draft for the chapter. Finally, David would like to thank Andy Genereux, the Mayor of Yamnuska, for providing enough beta, notes, criticisms, and florid narrative for three books this size. And of course, hugely, ultimately, necessarily ... Urs Kallen, who invented the place.

Ben Gadd wishes to thank archeologist Peter Francis, K-Country planner Don Cockerton, geologists Brian Pratt, Glen Stockmal and Jerry Osborne, GSC librarian John McIsaac, Stoney Band history expert Ian Getty, Trailminders member Bob Smith, and Diane and Mike McIvor.

Thank you to those who contributed photos and drawings: Gillean Daffern, Alan Kane, Lyn Michaud, Job Kuijt, Matthew Wheeler, the Whyte Museum of the Canadian Rockies, the Provincial Archives of Alberta and the Glenbow Archives.